HOW JENNA BECAME MY DILEMMA

KORTNEY KEISEL

First edition September 2023

Cover design by Melody Jeffries Design

www.kortneykeisel.com

To Nixon
Thanks for always being my snuggle buddy, for making us laugh, and for being the coolest kid around.
I love you.

CHAPTER ONE

THE PROMISED PRINCE PRESS DAY: LOS ANGELES

JENNA

"THANK you both for letting me interview you." Nina Gregory from *LA Buzz* stares back at us. She reminds me of someone with her candy-apple lipstick and creepy smile, but I can't quite place it.

"Thanks for being here," Cody answers while I say, "Of course."

We sit side by side in matching damask topaz chairs in a suite at the Four Seasons Hotel. This is hour six of the rotation, and my face hurts from smiling so much, but a press tour is important for the series and the premiere of episode one.

"Jenna, my first question is for you." Nina's brown eyes swing to me. "What's it like starring opposite Hollywood's hottest male actor, Cody Banner, in the series adaptation of the best-selling young-adult dystopian royal romance *The Promised Prince?*"

Why is this always the first thing interviewers ask me? Why doesn't she ask him what it's like starring opposite America's *current* top model? Cody shifts in his chair, and I feel his smug gaze on me. He *loves* this question. Has all day. But I ignore him and press my lips into a full smile, giving Nina the response she wants to hear.

"Working with Cody is absolutely delightful."

I don't miss his snicker.

JENNA: FOUR MONTHS AGO

"Can we go over blocking for this scene one more time? I just want to make sure it's cemented in my brain."

And because, honestly, I have no clue what I'm doing.

I thought my transition from modeling to acting would be easy. Walking up and down a runway involves portraying a certain persona. Acting was supposed to be an extension of that, but each day I arrive on set, I find I'm more and more out of my element and more unsure that I can actually break into acting.

Cody groans beside me, tipping his head back while dragging both hands down his face. "We've already been over blocking ten times."

Then there's Cody Banner.

He oozes with confidence and has little patience for people like me—people who aren't confident in acting and are just faking it 'til they make it.

But he can sense fear, so I lift my chin in his direction, hoping to fool him into thinking I'm in complete control. "And I'd like to go over it again."

"At this rate, I'll be eighty before we ever finish filming this scene. And honestly"—his smile perks in that smug way I've grown to despise—"I'm not sure eighty-year-old Cody will be as big of a hit with the ladies."

It takes fifty-nine days of doing something to create a habit. I've only been ignoring Cody for thirty-seven. That's easy math for an accounting major like me. I'm twenty-two days shy of it being a habit, but ignoring him already feels like second nature.

I glance at the director. "Quinton, do you want me standing here, or should I—"

"It's called acting," Cody interjects. "So just act. Don't overthink it. Just. Act."

"Oh, I'm sorry. Is my attention to detail bugging you?" I pair my sarcasm with a fake frown.

"I'm sure it's bugging everyone." Cody gestures around the set to the watching crew members.

Glaring at him doesn't adequately portray my annoyance, but that's my only weapon—well, that and my words.

"This kind of stuff"—my hands circle through the air, implying 'blocking'—"is what sets brilliant actors apart from mediocre ones. You should try it sometime. Then maybe you'd finally win a best actor award."

"Oh, sweetie, that's where you're wrong. This kind of stuff"—he mimics my hand motions—"is what separates amateur actors from professional ones. Maybe you should go back to being a supermodel if you can't—"

"Okay!" Quinton steps between us. "That's enough of that. Why don't you both take a little break before you kill each other?"

"Maybe I want to kill him." I throw him a smile that's way too sweet to ever be considered genuine.

NINA'S EYES are still on me. "Was *The Promised Prince* the first time you met Cody?"

"Yes," Cody quickly answers.

"No." My stony eyes flip to him. "I met him eight years ago at an after-party at Jennifer Lawrence's house."

"I don't think you can really call that *meeting* someone."

"Actually, he's right about that. More like we bumped into each other briefly."

Nina Gregory leans forward as if she's a teenage girl

getting the gossip about my boyfriend. "Was Cody every bit as charming as you imagined?"

I prefer not to imagine Cody in any capacity.

"Words can't even describe." There goes my big smile again, doing what it does best.

"What did you guys talk about back then?" She gets her pen ready, like I'm about to tell her the cutest story ever. "Can you remember the details?"

"You know, we didn't talk much."

"That's because I had my hands full."

"Yes, you did," I say under my breath while maintaining my smile.

JENNA: EIGHT YEARS AGO

Why did I drink so much Diet Coke?

Oh, I know.

Because I'm starving, and liquid is a better option than the trays of delicious hors d'oeuvres floating around the party. I'm sure one brie-and-prosciutto shortbread is at least three hundred and fifty calories—a hit I cannot afford with Fashion Week coming up. But now my bladder is paying for my attempt to fool my stomach into thinking I don't need food.

Sixth door on the right. That's where Jennifer said the upstairs bathroom is. There's been a hijacking of the downstairs bathroom by a couple working off their prosciutto shortbread with a hot and heavy makeout.

Three. Four. Five.

The door is cracked open, making it easy to hear what can only be described as female giggling. The giggles are followed by a man's short, choppy words.

"Whoa. Oh. No. Eh. No."

More high-pitched laughter. "Don'tcha like to be touched?"

"Depends on the night." His words come out in a rough spurt. "And it depends on the woman."

There's a stumble and noises. My mind takes those noises and fills in the blanks: two bodies slamming into the wall, plus something really heavy crashing to the ground and then rolling across the floor.

"Whatch about you and me tonightch?" Her words are tagged with a drunken slur from too much partying.

"Oh. Hey. Uh." Alarm coats each of his words.

More crashing and thrashing.

When did bathrooms turn into brothels instead of a place to relieve yourself?

My restroom needs can't wait any longer, so I push open the door, ready to face whatever indecency there is. The momentum of the door stops when it bangs into someone.

"Oh, boy!" the man grunts.

I peek my head in and watch the last moments of him falling on top of the woman lying on the floor by the toilet. There are a lot of arms and legs and just a general blob of bodies, so it's hard to tell what's happening.

But again, my mind can fill in the blanks well enough.

The woman's extremities lock around his body. "Thish ish more like it."

A wrestle takes place, and I can't tell if the man is initiating some kind of weird make-out position or trying to get off her.

"Do you two mind?" I say over them.

His head flips to me. I instantly recognize the azure eyes and swaggering smile that belong to Hollywood's most infamous player.

Cody Banner.

I'm actually not even surprised that he's on top of a woman in the bathroom. His reputation has preceded him.

"Come in. Join us," he says.

My brows jump to my hairline. "Excuse me?"

5

"There's room for three." Impish. That's how I'd describe his smile.

"I definitely won't be joining you two," I scoff. "And quite frankly, I'm offended that you'd imply I'm interested in—"

"Whoa, whoa! What are you talking about?" He attempts to crawl off the woman, but her legs link around his neck, putting him in a headlock. She must own a Thigh Master and use it regularly, because she's got an iron-clad hold on him. I half expect Cody to turn blue from lack of oxygen. Instead, he grabs her thighs and yanks, causing her to laugh and squirm. With her guard down, he's able to break free and stand. Instead of fixing his messy dark hair, he shakes his head at me. "I wasn't suggesting you join us like you think I was suggesting it. I was just making a joke about how small the bathroom is."

My hard gaze narrows on him. "Right."

"Look"—he steps over the woman whose legs have become scissors, slicing through the air in an attempt to trip him—"this isn't what you think. She had a little too much to drink, and I'm just trying to help her."

"Do you know her age, weight, how much, and how fast she drank tonight versus how much she ate?"

He laughs, and his blue eyes twinkle just like the little star in the nursery rhyme. "I have no clue."

I look the woman over. "She's probably about a hundred and ten pounds, and depending on how many drinks she's had per hour and the state she's in right now"—I do some quick math in my head—"I would say her blood-alcohol level is between .10 and .12 percent."

"Did you just figure that out in your head?"

"Yeah."

His stare stays on me as a dawn of recognition hits. "Aren't you that underwear model?"

"Ugh!" My eye roll makes a complete rotation. "Of course you'd only remember the underwear ads."

"Do you prefer I not remember them?"

The woman on the floor flops to her stomach with a harrumph. For a moment, it looks like she might fall asleep, but then her tongue shoots out, gliding back and forth over the tile.

My face twists in disgust. "I hope you already got your make-out in."

Cody's expression is stoic as he watches. "I wasn't planning on adding her to my rotation."

"Not an open spot?"

That same teasing smile appears. "Not for her. But if you want in, I'm sure I can make room."

"How generous of you."

"I like to think of myself as a pretty generous guy."

Our stares are broken up by vomiting hurls.

"Charming." My nose scrunches as I turn my head.

"At least she made it to the toilet."

Two more retches are followed by a long, drawn-out moan as the woman rests against the wall.

"Do you think you can take her now? I really need to use the restroom."

"Come on." Cody bends down, wrapping her arm around his shoulder. "Up she goes."

Once to her feet, she ducks out of Cody's arm and stumbles toward the door, turning back to face us. "Thanksh for showing me your Oshcar." I would've taken her comment to be dirty, except for the fact that Cody just won an actual Oscar tonight for his supporting role in Men in Flames. "I'd love to schee it again shometime." She attempts a wink, but it's more like a double-chin grimace with one eye closed. On her way out, she hits her head on the door jamb and disappears down the hall.

"She's a keeper." I whistle. "I hope you got her phone number for later. But in all seriousness, I didn't have the facts to calculate whether or not she's in danger of alcohol poisoning, so watch her closely."

"That's nice of you to be so concerned."

"Well, I don't want anything bad to happen to her."

"Don't worry. I'll make sure she gets home safe."

"I bet you will." There's a sarcastic bite behind my words.

Cody slowly approaches me. His nearness is a surprise, and I step back, hitting the open door against the wall.

"I told you. She's not in the rotation. I'm saving the spot for you."

My eyes dart back and forth across his face. Now that I'm looking directly at him, there are a few notable things worth mentioning. One: Cody Banner's short beard, angular jaw, and smooth skin are as exquisite up close as they are on the big screen. Two: he smells incredible. Maybe he wasn't born with sweat glands and, therefore, doesn't have the natural body odor you'd expect from a ten-hour night of partying and dancing (actually, I think we're on our eleventh hour of the night—award shows start crazy early). And three: there are two different shades of lipstick on his shirt collar, and I'm guessing neither belongs to the woman who just exited the bathroom.

His smile taunts and teases like it's his job to make women blush. My breaths are shallow, and all I want is to be free of him so I can breathe again.

"Unless you'd like more than vomit on your Armani shoes, I'd take your exit now."

He sniffs out a laugh before lazily leaning down like he's picking something up. My eyes drop to the side, following his outstretched hand. It's the freaking Oscar. He brought it with him to the bathroom like it's an inhaler or a tampon. I hadn't noticed it on the floor beside us, but there it is, in all its golden, chiseled-man glory.

"Don't want to leave this behind." He straightens, shaking the trophy in front of my face. "Apparently, it's a big deal."

His body turns as if he's finally going to leave, but then he stops. He leans in close, purposely tickling my neck with his words. "By the way, my shoes are Prada brushed leather. Not Armani."

My gaze holds his stare. "All the more reason not to get them wet."

Cody smiles, running his heated gaze across my face. Just when I feel like I'm about to melt under his stare, he resumes his strides, finally leaving me alone with my business.

"I'D LOVE to hear about when you two met up again for the second time to film *The Promised Prince*." Nina cuts through my daydream with her next question. "What was that like?"

A nightmare, Nina. It was like my worst nightmare.

My head shakes in perfect innocence. "It's nothing special. Just a boring story."

Cody turns his head to me with a dazzling smile. "It wasn't *that* boring."

CODY: FIVE MONTHS AGO

I lean forward, catching my driver's attention. "Can we stop on the way at Taco Bell or something? I'm starving."

"No." Dallas makes the decision from the passenger seat as if he's the superstar and I'm his publicity manager—a depressing role reversal. "We're already late to your first table read with the cast, and the entire point of doing this series is to improve your image. No one is going to take you seriously if you show up late on day one, holding a nacho cheese steak chalupa."

"What if I show up holding a nacho bell grande? Would that be okay?"

Dallas rolls his eyes, shifting his annoyance out the

window. But as soon as he settles, he straightens again in his uptight way. "There's a woman up ahead with car trouble." He cranes his neck, trying to see.

"So?"

"So I think we should pull over and help her." He points to the side of the highway so my driver knows.

"Now we have time to make a stop?" I glance out the window to the shoulder of the road. "Taco Bell was out of the question because we'd be late, but punctuality doesn't matter when we're helping someone?" The second I say it, I know how I sound. I'm all for helping people. Really, I am. And maybe afterward, we can get a taco party pack to celebrate our impromptu kindness.

We slowly pass a red BMW with a woman standing in front of a blown tire. Stopping twenty feet ahead of where her car is parked, Dallas looks at me expectantly.

"Oh, you want me to be the one who gets out and changes the tire? All the grease and dirty tire stuff. You want me to do that?"

"Yes, so I can film you helping and then leak it to the press."

And there goes the impromptu kindness.

"You're kidding me, right?"

"No." He fumbles with his phone like he's getting it ready. "My job is to change the narrative around you. We have to go from Hollywood's playboy to a mature, upstanding adult. So go fix the tire, and whatever you do, don't flirt with her."

"Why would I flirt with her?"

Dallas's eyes narrow in a don't-try-my-patience kind of way.

"Fine. I won't flirt with her. Geez." I step out of the car, not missing his warning glare.

I walk toward long, slender legs; blonde, wavy hair; flawlessly tanned skin; designer sunglasses; and a lot of natural perkiness under her white t-shirt.

Is this some kind of test?

Did Dallas plant the gorgeous woman with "car problems" just to see if I had it in me not to flirt? I wouldn't put it past him. When it comes to my image restoration, he's all in—much to my annoyance.

"What seems to be the problem here, ma'am?" My six-year-old self smiles at how much I sound like a police officer, and the added ma'am ticks off the no-flirting clause. You don't use ma'am when you're trying to impress a woman.

She turns, and her mouth hitches into a surprised smile. "This works out perfectly." She gestures to me. "It's you!"

I drop my chin in feigned modesty. "Yeah, I know. I get recognized a lot."

Her surprised smile morphs into something more akin to a frown. "I bet you do."

Since I can't flirt with her, there's no point in dilly-dallying, especially when I'm already running late. I crouch in front of her rim, giving Dallas his picture-perfect moment. "Looks like a blown tire." I glance up at the woman. "Do you have a spare?"

Light-brown eyebrows drop below the rim of her sunglasses, hiding from my view, but I still register the confused expression on her face. "You're going to try and fix it?"

"Yeah." Why do people think movie stars are incapable of doing normal things? Hasn't she seen the magazine spreads with pictures of famous people grocery shopping or cleaning up their dog's crap with the title 'Celebrities are Just Like Us'?

"Instead of taking the time to fix it, why not just give me a ride?"

"Uh." I laugh at her forwardness, adding a touch of a flirty smile—just a touch, but if Dallas has an angle, it'll be enough to make him upset. "I don't usually pick up women off the side of the road." I wink at her. "Safety reasons."

She folds her arms across her chest. "That's not what I've heard."

"You can't trust everything you read online."

She scoffs as if she doesn't believe me.

"Since stranger danger is a concern, let's just fix your tire." Can you imagine how angry Dallas would be if I brought the woman back to the car? Something like that goes way beyond flirting.

"Stranger danger?"

"Yeah." I shrug innocently, but secretly, I'm proud of my charm.

Her chin dips down, and there's a notable moment when her jaw hardens. "You don't know who I am, do you?"

"Uh…" My eyes squint up at her. Yes, she does look familiar, but with the big sunglasses, it's hard to see her entire face and place how we know each other. Plus, the sun is in my eyes. No one can see anything when the sun is in their eyes. She's beautiful enough that I'm sure I hit on her, and based on her irritated expression, it didn't end well. Who am I kidding? It never ends well with women I've dated. "Do we know each other?"

An angry puff bursts out. "You really don't recognize me?"

I slowly stand. "Of course I recognize you. It's just been so long I don't remember the details." Like her name, or how exactly I know her or—more importantly—wronged her.

The hardness in her jaw transfers to her cheeks—I'm guessing to her hidden eyes—and then up to her forehead.

I've done it now.

"You're exactly what I imagined." She flings open her car door and starts gathering her phone and purse. My brows lower in confusion as I watch her sharp movements. "Tawny said, 'Give him a chance. Maybe he's different.'" She laughs, something high and without humor. "But this solidifies everything." She slams the door and faces me. "I don't have to feel guilty. I just need to get in and get out."

I must've done a real number on this girl. And who the heck is Tawny?

"I'm sorry, I don't understand why you're so upset."

She tugs her purse strap over her shoulder and marches past me.

"Wait." I spin around, watching her stomp away. "Where are you going?"

"To work!"

Hands go to my hips as my head drops back. I gaze at the sky for a second, taking a deep breath before slowly bringing my head upright. My eyes stop on the giant billboard almost right above where I'm standing, and my head tilts. It's a Victoria's Secret ad with Jenna Lewis lying on her side in a silky gray nightie. Her head rests on her hand, and her long blonde hair cascades over her shoulders and chest.

I glance at the woman reaching for my door handle, and I know.

My entire body shrinks with embarrassment. "Oh, crap."

I run to her just as she opens my car door.

"Miss Lewis," Dallas says instantly, and she whips her head to me with satisfaction.

"Yes!" I gesture to her. "It's Jenna Lewis…my costar."

She takes off her sunglasses as she ducks into the car. "Can you give me a ride to the table read? I'll have my assistant take care of my car."

"Of course," Dallas says. "We're already going there. I'm so glad we stopped."

Jenna scoots to the other side of the backseat, making room for me to sit down. "Your client doesn't have a clue who I am."

Dallas's mortified gaze swings to me as I shut the door.

"She had sunglasses on," I defend before turning my head to her. "You had big sunglasses, and the sun was in my eyes.

Besides, I wasn't looking at your face. I was looking at your tire."

"Right." She laughs. "You didn't know who I was, but you expect everyone to know who you are."

"No, that's not true. I know who you are. There was a Victoria's Secret billboard of you right above us."

"So you're saying if I had been dressed in a bra and panties, you would've recognized me?"

"That's not what I'm saying at all." I brush my fingers over my beard. "Can we start over? I'm Cody Banner. It's nice to meet you."

She turns her head away. "We've already met before."

Dallas's eyes are drilling me from the front seat to fix this, so I change the subject.

"Are you nervous for today?" Small talk. Every good relationship starts with small talk.

"Why would I be nervous about the table read?"

"I just assumed you'd be nervous because this is your first time acting."

"I've acted before. My modeling career started with a Coca-Cola commercial, but I wouldn't expect you to remember that." She's smiling at me, but I get the sense it's a false positive.

"I remember the Coca-Cola commercial, but you weren't acting. You were posing…in a bikini." My brows lift, and my lips curve. Jenna's eyes narrow as if she's prepping for some chauvinistic comment about how good she looked in the bikini, but I'm not going to give her the satisfaction.

"You drank the heck out of that Coke."

She exhales, relaxing her expression. "I guess."

"Anyway, don't be nervous." My smile turns teasing, and I hope she picks up on it. "We can always put you in a bra and panties if things don't go well with your acting."

"I'm surprised they haven't tried that tactic with you yet. Maybe then you'd finally get a decent movie review."

I laugh, throwing my head back. "Touché."

Our disastrous beginning can be salvaged.

I'm sure of it.

JENNA

"NOW, let's get to the question everyone is dying to know." Nina lifts her shoulders in excitement, turning her eyes to me. "What was it like kissing Cody Banner? Were you nervous? I mean, he's kissed a lot of Hollywood's A-list actresses on and off the big screen?"

"Yes, I'm sure his kiss count is higher than the Himalayas."

"Very funny," Cody mutters.

"I wasn't nervous at all."

Cody chokes on his laugh, morphing it into a cough.

I raise my chin with perfect confidence. "It was all very professional."

JENNA: THREE MONTHS AGO

"CUT!" Quinton leaps out of his director's chair. His momentum and anger propel him forward until he's standing on the dock right in front of us. "Do you two even know how to kiss? Or how to pretend to kiss? Because this scene only calls for a peck. A peck!"

"I think we can all agree that I know how to kiss a woman." Cody's mouth hitches up at the corner. A multimillion-dollar celebrity brand was built off that exact smirk.

My jaw goes slack. "So do I."

"You know how to kiss a woman?" Blue eyes swing to me

as amusement rounds his smirk into a full smile. "I'd like to see that."

"You know what I mean, but you can't go two minutes without saying something inappropriate."

"And you can't make it through a simple kissing scene without breaking into hives. How many times have we had to stop and call makeup over to cover up the red blotches on your neck and arms? I lost count at sixteen or seventeen."

Yes, it's true.

I'm the girl with the skin rash.

I'm not proud of it.

But even though this is just a short kiss, I'm so nervous I can't help how my body is reacting. I'm vulnerable here, and nothing about the situation feels safe.

So, yeah, my body breaks into hives.

"What can I say?" My smile is sweet and innocent. "I'm so repulsed by the thought of kissing you that I involuntarily break out in hives whenever you come near."

"I'm not thrilled about kissing you either, and that's saying a lot for a man who has a reputation in the tabloids of being 'extremely experienced with women.'"

"Well, for someone so experienced, you should've known not to eat a garlic-tuna-fish sandwich right before a kissing scene. I can smell your breath six feet away. Real impressive."

"Trust me. You're the last woman in the world I'm trying to impress. But I only ate the sandwich because I thought we were filming a different scene."

"One kiss!" Quinton yells. "That's all I need to make this meet-cute scene work, and then you two can go back to hating each other until episode five, when—unfortunately for all of us—you have to kiss again." He looks at Cody. "So get a breath mint." He looks at me. "Take some Benadryl. And let's get this horrific kiss over with."

16

"TOMORROW IS the red-carpet premiere of episode one of *The Promised Prince*, where I'm sure you and Cody Banner will dazzle fans with your on- and off-screen chemistry. How could you not?" Nina's smile holds, and the spark of recollection finally lights my brain. Her creepy, wide smile with her too-bright red lipstick reminds me of The Joker from *Batman*. Slap some white paint all over her face, and the resemblance is uncanny. "I mean, look at you two." Her gaze bounces between us. "You're the sexiest man alive, and you're an international supermodel. I can only imagine how the sparks fly between you two."

"Oh, there are sparks." Cody sucks in. "That's for sure."

"So many sparks." I hope Nina doesn't notice the dryness behind my words.

"Is there any chance you two might become more than just costars? Maybe bring some of that explosive chemistry into your personal lives?"

"No." Cody shakes his head.

Disappointment crosses over her face. "No?"

"No." My answer is final and resolute.

CHAPTER
TWO

CODY

DALLAS WAITS on the curb as my stretch Benz pulls up to the red-carpet premiere of *The Promised Prince*. My publicity manager shines in a sleek black suit instead of his usual navy Dockers and collared white shirt. I swear his wife showed up at L.L. Bean one day and bought three-hundred-and-sixty-five sets of his signature outfit so he didn't have to compromise his "look" for the sake of laundry. But at least for tonight, he has mixed things up a little.

Dallas Mikesell wasn't my first choice for a manager, but he's one of the best in the business at making a celebrity likable after they've fallen out of good graces, which is exactly where I find myself. Ten years ago, when I came on the scene, I made some stupid, youthful mistakes. I didn't start as a serious actor who demonstrated maturity. I prioritized having fun over everything else and got the reputation as the guy who likes partying, drinking too much, uncommitted relationships, shameless flirting, and breaking women's hearts. I top all of Hollywood's playboy lists.

But a person can only sustain that kind of lifestyle for so long. In your twenties, it's considered cute. In your thirties, you're a bad influence on society. If I want my acting career to actually last, I need to turn the tide on how the public sees me. That's where recently hired Mr. L.L. Bean comes in.

Dallas is step one toward image restoration.

"Are you ready to have hundreds of obsessed women scream at you?" My assistant, Julio, looks at me from across the car.

"It's what I live for." The languid expression on my face contradicts my words.

"Well, you look the part, and I'll be waiting with the car once the event is over."

I nod at Julio, then smooth my suit pants and tug on the matching pale-pink Gucci jacket—yes, pink. A fitting choice for my first full-blown romance movie premiere. Actually, this isn't a movie. It's a premiere for episode one. I'm working for television now—a *Flixmart Original Series*. This is all part of the image restoration. I'm transitioning into lovable acting roles that are crucial to making me seem charismatic and charming in my old age.

I'm thirty.

Apparently, that's ancient in Hollywood.

So we're in this strange transition phase from boy to man, even though I'm already a man...an *old* man.

Celebrity publicity is weird like that.

At least I get to play a prince in the show. And there are a few light action scenes. Those are the *only* redeeming things about this project. I'm used to starring in blockbuster movies where stuff gets blown up. I don't portray men whose entire character is centered around falling in love. Why not cut off my manhood right now?

But that was the old Cody.

The new Cody wears pink suits and stars in dystopian royal romances.

Paparazzi not invited to the event snap pictures as I step

out of the car. Questions fire at me in rapid succession from different photographers.

"Cody, are you alone at the premiere tonight?"

"Is Calista James joining you?"

"Are you the reason she and Billie Francom are getting a divorce?"

"Cody, have you been in rehab?"

I will never understand the rehab question whenever I disappear from the public eye. For the last month, I was in the Maldives, soaking up the sun, escaping from my real-life problems and the recent Calista James rumors. If there's anything I do well, it's avoid real feelings. When the going gets tough, I don't get tougher. I run while *looking* tough. It makes for a way less complicated life.

I'm surprised none of the paparazzi notice my tan. Where are their sleuthing skills on that one? A better question would've been, *'Cody, did you use Hawaiian Tropic lotion to get a bronze that deep?'* That's the real story here.

Dallas steps forward, shielding me as I drop my head and move toward the safety of the celebrity tent. Water and fans keep the A-list guests cool inside as they wait for their turn to walk the red carpet.

"You showing up solo tonight doesn't help with the Calista James story." Dallas shoves a cold water bottle into my hand.

"I already told you. There is no Calista James story."

I mean, there *is*, but not in the way Dallas thinks.

"I really don't care if there is or isn't. I just care what the public thinks, and a relationship with a *married* Calista James is not going to help you, especially if people think you're the reason she's separated from her husband. What we need is a decoy relationship with a good girl."

"A decoy relationship?" I'm not even trying to hide my annoyance with this idea.

"Yeah, something to take the buzz off you and Calista, just for now, until her divorce is finalized."

"There's no buzz," I say again. "You don't need to worry about it."

"No, you don't need to worry about it. I'll take care of everything."

I'm starting to get annoyed. "There's nothing to take care of."

He looks me over with a frown. "Why are you still wearing your sunglasses? Please don't tell me you've already started drinking for the night, and now your eyes are too bloodshot for pictures."

I slowly turn my neck, looking at him *through* my glasses. I extend my arm out and raise my hand to the rims, dramatically pulling the sunglasses off my face. My gaze narrows, giving him a good look at my sober and clear blue eyes before I hold the sunglasses out for him to take.

"Phew! We just can't make any mistakes today. This red-carpet event is big for your image." He grabs the sunglasses, tucking them inside his suit pocket. "But you know I had to ask. It wouldn't be the first time you showed up to a premiere drunk." He offers that last part as an excuse for jumping to conclusions.

One time.

I showed up drunk to a premiere *one time*, three years ago, and it wasn't even my movie premiere, but the moment lives in infamy. And it's not like I did anything crazy. I stumbled a few times and yelled across the red carpet to Stacy Starrey, but my speech was so slurred that no one knew what I was trying to say.

Britney, Lindsay, and Paris did *waayy* worse stuff than that during their destructive prime.

But the tabloids blamed my drunken outburst on reckless, all-day-and-all-night partying. Not true unless you consider clearing out a storage facility after your estranged mother's death a party.

I do not.

Dallas Mikesell means well. His efforts would mean more if he actually believed I was a good guy or at least believed I could change into a good guy. But I guess I need to prove that to him first.

"Well"—I slap him on the back, a cue that I'm ditching this conversation—"that's why I pay you the big bucks. To make me look good no matter what."

I leave him and walk around the star-studded holding tent, greeting people.

"Cody." Teague Morrow nods at me, then drops his eyes down my suit. A small smile touches his lips. "Pink? Interesting choice. I wouldn't have worn it, but you always do your own thing."

If I'm Hollywood's bad boy, then Teague Morrow is their golden child. Every romantic-comedy role goes to him. Women love his dimples, charming personality, and never-ending smile. He plays my best friend, Drake, in the show, which is fitting since he's the closest thing I have to a friend in real life. If *The Promised Prince* does well, Flixmart will make book two into season two, and Teague will become the main character of the show for that season.

"Teague, I wouldn't expect you to understand style." I glance around. "Your wife's not joining you?"

"She decided to stay home. Our baby is due in a couple of weeks."

"That's right. I can't believe you're going to be a dad."

"Between all your women and partying, I wouldn't expect you to comprehend something like that. I almost envy your freedom, but I love my wife too much for that."

And I envy your settled-down family life.

My brows drop. That's a weird thought to have. It completely came out of left field, making it easy for me to brush away.

"You, of all people, know that women and partying aren't

all they're cracked up to be. Besides, I haven't been in that scene for a long time."

"Yeah, right." His neck kicks back in disbelief. "You *are* that scene."

Why is that always the narrative? *Cody Banner, the wild partier.* It's not like I was the only person at those Hollywood parties back in the day, but I'm usually the only person whose name ended up in the tabloids.

"You know it wasn't that long ago that you were right there with me, living that same lifestyle."

"Eh"—Teague eyes me with a smirk—"we all have to grow up sometime."

"Tell me about it."

For some of us, the transition is much more difficult. Take Teague, for example. He's never been labeled as a playboy or a bad boy, even though his early years in Hollywood mimicked mine. He's gotten a hall pass because of his dimples and boy-next-door smile and all the cinnamon-roll heroes he's played in films, while I have to reinvent myself and my career just to gain some respect.

But he's the golden boy, and golden boys never have to work as hard to be liked.

When Dallas was brainstorming ways I could restore my image, his was the first name he brought up. Said if I really wanted to win people over, I needed to pattern myself off Teague Morrow. But even as Dallas said that, I saw the doubt in his eyes, like he didn't think I could ever be *that* guy, no matter how good at spinning stories he is.

"Are you nervous about the showing tonight?" Teague takes another sip of his water. "Romantic series aren't your typical genre. Heck, I didn't even know it was in your wheelhouse."

"Everything is in my wheelhouse."

"Maybe." His smile is more friendly than smug. "We'll have

to wait and see what the press and fans think about the show. If the response isn't good, it complicates everything. A streaming series is a lot different than a movie. There's the added pressure of episodes releasing each week on Flixmart *while* you finish filming the last few episodes of season one. There's a lot riding on this for all of us. Are you sure you can handle the pressure?"

"You don't have to worry about me or the show. This isn't my first rodeo."

"But it's hers." His gaze travels across the tent.

For the first time tonight, I see Jenna. She stands out in a fitted red dress, a nod to the iconic red-dress scene we'll film sometime in the next week and a half. Her blonde hair is slicked into an elegant bun with some kind of droopy side-bang thing happening in the front. I might not know how to describe the specifics of her dress and hair, but I can describe how she looks—absolutely memorable.

"What?" I shrug. "You haven't been impressed with Jenna on the show?"

"She's really nice, but she should probably stick to modeling." Teague laughs. "It's cute these days how everyone thinks they can act."

I frown. "Jenna *can* act."

"Come on. She's just another pretty face."

Jenna and I have had our differences for the last five months, but that doesn't mean I want her to fail at acting. To be honest, I don't even know why we don't get along. I started the project thinking we'd be a great fit. But on day one, she showed up with a chip on her shoulder, probably because I didn't know who she was. But after that, she didn't even try to forgive me or get to know me. She'd already decided, from what she'd heard around town, that she didn't like me. So the rivalry began. But right now, none of that seems to matter. Yes, she has a pretty face—she has a pretty *everything*—but she's also talented. Better than some actresses who've been in the business for twenty years (not that I would ever admit that to her).

"Jenna works hard, takes copious notes, implements *all* of Quinton's suggestions"—much to my annoyance—"and dives deep into her character. She'll end up being one of Hollywood's most sought-after actresses. You're wrong about her. Just wait and see."

I have no clue where this protectiveness is coming from, but it's rearing its ugly head like someone just insulted my little sister. Yeah, sure…this is a big-brother kind of protectiveness. Let's go with that reasoning, because any other doesn't make sense.

"It's not like you to hand out compliments." The amusement in Teague's smile kicks up a notch. "If I hadn't seen you two together on set, I would've thought there was something going on between you."

"I don't mix business and pleasure."

"You definitely don't with her, that's for sure." He laughs. "But maybe if you did, you'd both start getting along. Or are you just too in love with Calista James to even see anyone else?"

"Those are just rumors."

"I bet." His gaze shifts around just for the show of it. "Where is Calista anyway? Shouldn't she be here with you?"

"Like I said, rumors."

"Teague"—a woman in all black with a headset smashing the bun on top of her head gently taps his forearm—"you're next on the red carpet."

He tugs his lapels. "I'll see you in there."

"Sounds good."

I scan the room, looking for someone new to talk to. My gaze lands on Jenna again and lingers. She's talking to her family. It's easy to see the resemblance between her and her parents, plus I recognize her famous NFL brother and his sportscaster fiancée. I come to these events alone while she has an entire support group cheering her on. The paradox between our two lives knocks me in the face.

How much different would things have been if I'd had even one person in my corner? One person at the beginning of my career to tell me the partying was getting out of hand. Maybe I wouldn't be standing here today, trying to reinvent myself. But those aren't the cards I was dealt. I shake the fleeting thought away because I'm about twelve years past caring about stuff like that.

JENNA

"JENNA! OVER HERE!"

I turn my face to the right, where the shouts came from. Sparks of light explode at me like the Fourth of July.

A slight smile.

A toe pop.

A shoulder tilt.

A dip of my chin.

It's all about angles.

I repeat it again on the other side.

"Jenna! Jenna!" Yelling photographers and camera flashes barely faze me anymore.

The woman in black with the badge around her neck and the clipboard in her hands ushers me forward to my next photo op.

As I slowly walk, my lips press together in a subtle slash of a smile, giving each press outlet the perfect front-page picture.

I own this red carpet.

Something about wearing a beautiful dress and having professional hair and makeup gives me an extra boost of I-can-do-this.

This is a big night for me.

My acting debut.

If I think about it too long, I'll curl up in the fetal position and rock back and forth. So I'm not going to think about it. I'm going to stand here and pretend like I'm the most confident woman in the world. I've been wearing that mask for so long no one knows it's just a facade.

"*Entertainment Live* with Ike Rosa is your next interview." Thank goodness for the woman with the clipboard guiding me, or else I'd never remember all these names.

"Jenna, you look stunning!" Ike gushes.

"Thank you." My smile beams as I take Ike by the hands and pull him to me, lightly pressing my cheeks against each of his.

"Your dress is gorgeous. Who are you wearing?" He shoves a microphone in front of me.

"Oscar de la Renta."

"Amazing!" His lips quirk. "We're at the LA premiere of your first stint in show business. How are you feeling right now?"

"It's very exciting, a bit surreal, and a little nerve-racking. But there's nowhere else I'd rather be."

"A few minutes ago, I caught up with your brother, NFL wide receiver Trey Lewis. He couldn't be prouder of his baby sister's debut on the big screen."

"Trey and my entire family have been so supportive during this shift from modeling to acting." That's not entirely true. My dad said I was making a massive mistake and that it would all blow up in my face, but Ike Rosa doesn't need to know that.

"Tell us about your role in *The Promised Prince*."

"I play Renna Degray, a common woman who ends up falling for her stepsister's betrothed, the prince."

"Did you see any of yourself in Renna's character?"

"Yes, probably too much at times." I laugh. "Not the part

about falling in love with a prince, but I related to her feeling like a fish out of water. She's in a new kingdom, trying to find who she is and where she belongs. I've felt that way a lot with my transition to acting."

"I bet." Ike nods. "*The Promised Prince* is a forbidden romance between Renna and Trev, who happens to be played by the uber-talented Cody Banner."

"That's correct."

Here come all the Cody questions. It's like they politely ask about me, biding their time until they can really talk about him.

"Speaking of Cody Banner." Ike shifts his gaze to Cody coming down the carpet behind me.

He looks absolutely devastating in his tailored, pale-pink suit with the top two buttons of his white shirt undone, giving every woman a peek at his tanned chest. I would admire his bold fashion choice if it weren't for the fact that it directly clashes with my red dress—a dead giveaway that we're *not* on the same page in the show or in real life.

"Cody, join us." Ike waves him over.

Great. Let's make this all about him.

"Jenna and I were just talking about the onscreen romance between your two characters." Ike gestures to me. "How was it playing the part of a man who's forbidden to be attracted to this goddess of a woman?"

"Most difficult role of my life," he deadpans. The double meaning behind his words is easy to catch if you know what to look for. "I mean, look at her." A charming smile pulls to me. "What man can resist this beauty? On- or off-screen."

What an actor!

I'm slow-clapping in my mind for his Oscar-worthy performance.

"This just makes me even more excited for the premiere. Will we see your characters interact much in episode one?"

I need to take back control of *my* interview. "Well, every

29

good romance starts with a meet-cute." Ours was more like a meet-hate, but we pulled it together for the sake of the show.

Cody laughs in his happy-go-lucky way. "That's how you know you're filming a romance—when words like *cute* are attached to everything. I wouldn't be surprised if, next, we filmed a fight-cute or a bathroom-break-cute."

Ike cackles, and I even see the cameraman's lips curve upward. In true Cody Banner style, he has these people eating out of the palm of his hand with his effortless charisma.

The woman with the clipboard motions that time's up.

"Well, I can't wait to see how it all plays out in the premiere of episode one."

We both give our thanks and continue down the carpet.

"You look nice." Cody's eyes dance up and down my body.

"As do you." My words come out curt, which is weird, considering they're a compliment. But I've learned with him you have to be on your guard at all times. If you let your walls down, he'll have you in love with him two seconds later and in his rearview mirror two seconds after that. A place I do not want to be. Because men like Cody never love you back. It's all just a game to them. They'll drop you as soon as they've won you.

The width of his smile increases. "I wore this color just for you."

"That's too bad since it clashes with my red dress." I keep my calm expression intact for the cameras even though my mind is wondering who his source is. Usually, my stylist team is pretty tight-lipped regarding my red-carpet apparel. But clearly, he knew and chose to wear something that didn't match. "But you probably did it to annoy me."

"Why would you think that?" He momentarily breaks eye contact with the cameras for a quick glance at me.

"Because you love to irritate me."

"No, men in pink don't try to irritate people." His head

dips close, sending shivers down the length of my spine with his whispers. "We're lovers, not fighters." He winks once before facing the crowd again.

It takes me one second to recover, but even in that short period of time, I'm worried someone caught my falter on camera.

"Cody! Jenna! Give us one together!"

Most people lean in, maybe tilt their heads when they're getting their picture taken with someone. Not us. Not me. We stand like two individual statues whose flesh will melt off our bodies if it touches the other person's. At least, that's how I stand. I do my best to relax my smile even though I feel the tenseness between us all the way down to my glittered shoes.

"Interesting idea to wear pink and red," a photographer shouts.

Great! Everyone else notices our lack of outfit coordination.

"They're the colors of love." Cody slips his hand behind my back. It's a light touch—like he's testing the waters—but it's there, causing my body to stiffen even more. "This is a romance series, isn't it?"

More smiles from the crowd. For a man they *love* to hate, they sure love him.

"Let's get the rest of the cast and crew in there." The clipboard woman waves over Quinton, Teague, and some of the side characters.

Cody and I split apart, making room for everyone else. We end up on opposite ends of the photos, like the bread on a sandwich.

And I finally feel like I can relax again and enjoy the moment.

CHAPTER
THREE

JENNA

I'M MORE nervous today than when I did an all-day photo shoot in the ocean with nurse sharks swimming around me.

Sharks.

Swimming around me.

While I was menstruating.

I was convinced the whole time that they would smell the blood and come take a bite out of my leg—or worse, my crotch. (Gross, I know. A mind just goes where it wants to go. I blame it on the nerves.)

Nurse-shark level of anxiety doesn't even come close to what I feel right now as I wait for my publicity manager to show up with the early reviews from last night's premiere.

I can usually scrape together some confidence. You have to if you want to make it as a model. People constantly judge your figure and how you look—while wearing practically nothing—so you learn to develop somewhat of a thick skin.

But no one's critiquing how I look.

It's all about how talented I am.

That feels a lot more personal.

And suddenly, my thick skin is gone. It's more like a sheer covering that will split open with any amount of pressure or criticism. So that's great.

Tawny knocks twice, and I rush to the door. Since she buzzed the gate at the end of my drive, I've been doing everything I can not to run outside and tackle her for the information. I fling open the door. My green eyes probably look crazed with a mixture of fear and cautious excitement.

"Have you seen the reviews yet?" Tawny walks past me and heads for my living room like she owns the place.

"No. You told me not to Google anything without you present." I quickly shut the door and run after her, trying to glean something from her facial expression.

"I didn't think you'd actually listen to me."

I'm a rule follower to a fault. Of course, I obeyed.

She drops onto my pristine white couch, reaching into her Chanel bag for a stack of papers. The roots of her brown hair show silver as if she hasn't had time to get into the salon for a touch-up. One leg crosses over the other. Then her brown eyes look at me. "You should sit for this."

That feels ominous.

I sink down across from her, swallowing back the anxiety rising.

"Let's start with the positive. Everyone agrees you looked exquisite in the show. Your face was made for the big screen."

My shoulders slowly deflate like an air mattress that's been pricked with a pin. "That's not a positive. I always get complimented on my looks. I want to know what they thought about my acting. Did they like *me*? Think *I* have talent?"

I'm not sure why it means so much to me to have someone think I'm talented for more than just looking good or walking on a runway in a nice dress, but it does mean a lot.

Impatience stretches across the lines of Tawny's crow's feet. "I'm getting to if they liked you."

"Right, sorry."

"They thought you embodied Renna perfectly. And there were even a few glowing reviews about your comedic delivery with the banter and how outstanding that was."

"That's great." Relief seeps out with my words.

"Yes, all good things."

"And what did they think of the show? I mean, I know it was only episode one, but did they like the storyline? Feel like it followed the book as much as they wanted it to?"

"Yes, the book fans loved the film adaptation so far. The setting, the costumes, the cinematography were all very well received."

A bright smile covers my entire face. I don't know what I was so worried about.

"So it's going to be a hit?"

"Not exactly." Tawny's lips pucker. "I haven't told you the negative yet." Her dramatic silence accentuates each pounding beat in my chest. "Critics hated you and Cody. Said you had zero chemistry. One even said he'd rather watch paint dry than watch the two of you together."

My back falls against the couch as if the weight of my plummeting heart forcefully pushed me there. "But the first episode was the meet-cute. We did all the flirty banter and even kissed."

"The kiss was average at most. I know it was only a peck, but it wasn't good. Bless Quinton and the producer's hearts. They did the best they could with what you gave them to work with, but it wasn't enough."

"This is only episode one. The chemistry builds throughout the series," I defend. "What do these people expect?"

"They expected explosive chemistry from the get-go, just like in the book. Cody is a Hollywood heartthrob known for his charm with the ladies, and you're, well…"—she waves her hand in front of me—"you're *you* in all your supermodel glory. I think people wanted the chemistry to match the sexiness you both exude. To be so hot that the screen would catch on fire."

My lips hover in a frown. "That's not even possible."

"It doesn't matter if it's possible. That's what they want."

"You both delivered the lines, and the acting was fine, but everyone agrees that something was missing. The *it* factor between you two. The chemistry."

"Well, these are just early reviews. I'm sure things will get better, especially if people like the story and the acting. We can change the tide with the chemistry. We haven't even filmed the last three episodes yet."

"Honey, I've seen you and Cody together. How are you going to magically turn on chemistry when you two hate each other?"

"By *acting*?"

Tawny pauses. "Is that a question?"

"Maybe." The skin on my nose crinkles.

"Unfortunately, I don't think the acting will carry us. Denzel, Will, McConaughey…none of them could pull off that level of acting. A key component of chemistry is vulnerability, and for some reason, neither you nor Cody feels safe enough to be vulnerable in front of the other. You both shut down, leaving no chance for a genuine relationship."

Tawny's right. Nothing about Cody Banner makes me feel safe. I could never trust him with my vulnerability. I'd rather gain one hundred pounds than let him see my uncertainty.

"It's not just the show," Tawny keeps going. "People are talking about how stiff the two of you looked on the red carpet last night, how you wouldn't pose together for pictures, and how, when you did talk, it appeared tense. There's speculation that things aren't going well behind the scenes."

"That's because they *aren't* going well behind the scenes."

"Well, now everyone knows."

"So? Plenty of actors haven't gotten along during filming. This is nothing new."

"Yes, but in this case, everyone's expectations were high because this is a best-selling book with beloved characters, and now that they've been let down, it's bleeding into their opinion of the show."

"How is this happening?" I fall forward, dropping my head into my hands. "How did I end up working with the one man in the world I can't stand?"

"Don't panic. I can devise some kind of spin to counteract the bad reviews. Maybe we could pin it all on Cody. Say he was drunk or something."

I lift my head, giving her a pointed stare.

"What?" She flips her hair back. "I thought that was a good plan."

"I'm not trying to ruin anyone's career. For the show to do well, both of us need to be likable."

"Fine. I'll think about it and come up with something else. Maybe Dallas Mikesell and his team will have some ideas. We can ask them tomorrow. Make it a group effort between our two camps."

"I don't even want to show up for filming tomorrow." I slump into the couch cushions. "How am I supposed to work when everyone hates the show?"

"No one hates the show. They just hate you and Cody together."

After working with Tawny for the last ten years, you'd think I'd be used to her bluntness, but it still takes me by surprise.

"Oh, don't look at me like that," she scoffs. "Nobody feels sorry for you. Even if *The Promised Prince* is a bust, you're still a supermodel. And you have a great butt."

"What?" My brows lower into a V. "That doesn't solve anything."

"It solves everything! If I had your butt, I'd walk around naked every day."

"That's the stupidest thing I've ever heard. You wouldn't walk around naked."

"I would. All day. Every day." Her expression remains serious. "Do you know what the rear end of a fifty-two-year-old woman looks like when her only cardio is walking to the refrigerator?" She leans to the side, raising her thigh and half her behind in the air. "Well, I do, and it isn't pretty. It's flabby and flat—droopy like it had some kind of stroke. A butt stroke. That's what it looks like."

A crack of a smile threatens to break open across my mouth. "I didn't know butt strokes were possible."

"Oh, they're possible. I'm living proof." She shifts her body back to her normal sitting position. "So, like I said, nobody's going to feel sorry for you. But don't worry. Somehow, I'll fix this whole no-chemistry thing."

No chemistry with the playboy.

I can't believe that's what I'm getting nailed for, especially when you look at my dating track record. My history includes a lineup of men exactly like Cody Banner.

Take my last boyfriend, for example. Ben Jackson. He was a walking red flag of uncommitted relationships, a never-ending bachelor who couldn't commit, while also being deliciously irresistible. I broke up with him because he wasn't all in—at least not with me—and at that moment, I vowed never to be interested in a man like that again.

But one vow doesn't erase the fact that I'm a sucker for the serial-dating flirt, and everyone knows it. That's probably why news outlets have shipped Cody and me ever since it was announced we'd be working together.

But I refuse to be another Hollywood cliché. I swore to myself months ago that Cody Banner would not get the best of me.

So maybe I'm to blame for the lack of chemistry between us. Maybe I've taken my vow too far. I'd already decided before filming even started that I wanted nothing to do with him. When it comes to our working relationship, my walls are so high Cody didn't even stand a chance.

And now my entire acting career is paying for it.

Fabulous.

Just fabulous.

CHAPTER
FOUR

CODY

"RYAN GOSLING and Rachel McAdams hated each other on the set of *The Notebook.*" Quinton's fists bang onto the table as he enunciates each word. "Hated. Each. Other. I was there, working as the director's assistant. And look what came of that movie—chemistry for days. That's what I want here. Chemistry! Chemistry! Chemistry!" He bangs the table again, causing Jenna to jump beside me.

Green screen filming in the studio is supposed to start in thirty minutes, but Quinton had things to say to me and Jenna that couldn't wait. As the director of *The Promised Prince,* he can do whatever he wants, including having a private discussion in his trailer. But this is starting to feel more like a drug intervention than a brainstorming session on how to bump up our early reviews.

A vein on Quinton's forehead bulges. "I want so much chemistry between you two that the United States government asks to convert our set into a state-of-the-art chemistry lab!"

"A chemistry lab?" The corner of my mouth rises. "I don't think—"

41

"Don't speak." Dallas's hand presses against my shoulder as he subtly shakes his head. "It's not helpful."

Snide comments are never helpful—always amusing but never helpful—so I keep my thoughts to myself.

"Even if these two"—Jenna's publicity manager gives us a stern side-eye glare—"can figure out how to conjure up some chemistry moving forward, that doesn't help the bad reviews that have already surfaced for episode one and are sure to come for episodes two and three."

"I talked with the producers and post-production team about the next two episodes, and we think their lack of chemistry might go unnoticed." Quinton's forehead vein relaxes, making it easier to follow what he says. Before, it was like he had a third eyeball staring at me. "These episodes are when Renna discovers Trev is engaged to her stepsister, and her anger and avoidance of him ramps up. So at least the bickering between their characters will feel authentic."

"See?" I lean back casually, lifting my hands in the air. "I don't know what we're all so worried about. There's no problem."

"That's not entirely true." Tawny (I think that's her name; I can't remember, and now it's been too many months to ask again) shifts her gaze to me. "We still need to do damage control on the criticism from the premiere this week."

"I thought we looked great." I consider winking at Jenna but decide against it after assessing the death glare aimed at me.

"You two were a disaster." Dallas opens a folder and slips pictures of us from the premiere onto the table. There are a few with us smiling and touching, but the touching looks forced and tense. I never would've pictured the day that touching a woman didn't come naturally to me, but Jenna is a whole different ballgame.

I'm attracted to her while simultaneously being scared of her. I don't care about her opinion of me, but deep down, I desperately want her to like me. I want her to think I'm a good actor, but I can't seem to open myself up and let go while filming. So yeah, the touching last night was forced and tense.

Dallas drops five more pictures in front of us, all with glares or frowns or both from Jenna pointed at me. I don't think I've ever had a woman dislike me so much—well, at least not when I haven't kissed her and then ditched her.

"Alright, well, do whatever you have to do to fix this." I wave the pictures away with my hand before standing. "Now, can we get started with filming?"

"Not so fast." Quinton motions for me to sit back down. "We're not filming any scenes with you two in them this weekend. We'll reschedule all of them for the Calgary location."

"Uh…" I laugh, glancing over at Jenna, who's been uncharacteristically silent during this whole intervention. "Is this, like, a timeout or something? Punishment because a few critics say we don't have on-screen chemistry?"

"I agree with those critics," Quinton snaps.

I actually do too.

It was painful watching the show last night. I cringed during our on-screen kiss, which has never happened to me before. Usually, I'm proud of my acting work, but everything about this project feels different—and not in a good way. I just can't get in a groove with Jenna.

"Until you two figure out your chemistry, I'm not filming any scenes with you together. Too many important moments are coming up: the ballroom scene, the red dress, the kiss. Your chemistry will make or break the entire show."

Talk about pressure.

"But I know what we need to do." Quinton's expression lightens, although it doesn't alleviate any pressure. Everyone stares back at him, waiting for the big reveal.

"You two will spend the weekend together at my beach house in Malibu."

Jenna chokes on a laugh. "I'm sorry. What?"

Looks like she can talk after all.

Quinton's focus turns to her. "I want you two to leave this afternoon and drive to my private beach house in Malibu."

"Why?" Jenna sounds like a teenage girl who just got her curfew moved up from midnight to ten o'clock.

"So you both can get to know each other better."

"The last thing we need is to spend more time together," Jenna whines, and I'm mildly offended by her adamant rejection of Quinton's plan. "We already know each other. We've been working together for months."

"No, you *tolerate* each other, which isn't the same as knowing."

Jenna smiles sweetly, as if she means to use her charm to get what she wants. "We don't need to spend the weekend together in Malibu. We can put our differences aside for work. We'll try harder to get along. We'll make an effort to get to know each other. But we can do that while we're filming. There's no need to go out of town."

Quinton leans back in his chair, folding his arms across his chest. "I'm not asking you. I'm telling you. I should've had you do this months ago when I first noticed you weren't getting along. But I'm doing it now. You'll go to Malibu together for the weekend, your assistants will book you new flights to our on-location filming site in Calgary, and you'll meet up with the rest of the cast on Monday."

A strained breath puffs out of Jenna's throat. "I can't just pick up and leave for Malibu."

Tawny's chin lifts. "I've spoken to Winnie. She's already packed your bag and brought it to the set."

Her jaw drops. "You knew about this?"

"We all did."

"Julio has a bag packed for you and is en route with your car."

I nod, impressed with Dallas's forethought.

"Wait." Jenna holds her hands up like she's stopping the conversation. "We're leaving now? From here? *Together?*"

"Yes." A no-nonsense look on Quinton's face keeps her from arguing further. So, instead, her green eyes whip to me.

"I can't believe you're okay with this."

"You heard Quinton. We don't have a choice. So why throw a tantrum about it?"

"I don't see why this is necessary."

"And I don't see why you care so much. You're being asked to spend a relaxing weekend in Malibu. Such a hard life."

Her jaw tightens as her glare falls over me. "A relaxing weekend *with you.*"

I'm a tough guy. Some would say a manly man. Sticks and stones aren't going to break my bones. It's words—specifically, *Jenna's* words—that surprisingly hurt me. But I do what I do best and use innuendo to cover up the sting.

"Are you scared to be alone with me? Afraid you'll end up having *too much* chemistry and liking it?"

She leans closer, lowering her voice to an intimate level. "Actually, I'm afraid I'll end up killing you and liking it."

My smile loosens as I hold her fiery glare.

Who says we don't have any chemistry?

JENNA

I GRAB my purse and loop it over my shoulder as I push open my trailer door and head down the metal stairs onto the asphalt. "You packed my moisturizer?"

Winnie follows, towing my suitcase. The wheels hit each step with a hard thud, making me glance behind to confirm she's not dragging a dead body. Nope. Just Louis Vuitton —*luggage*, not the French designer.

45

"I have your moisturizer and your new eyelash serum."

"What about *The Promised Prince* script?"

"I thought this wasn't a work weekend."

I stop walking and turn to look at her. I'm still getting used to Winnie's auburn hair. It's usually a light-brown shade, but I had my stylist dye her hair darker last week. It's a good look, complementing the light spray of freckles that covers the bridge of her nose and cheekbones.

"It's not a work weekend, but since I have nothing to say to Cody, I thought I could fill a bit of time by memorizing my lines."

"Got it. As in, I understand why you need your script, and also, I already packed it." My assistant's attention to detail is lifesaving.

"Thank you." I lead the way to the parking lot, where I'm supposed to meet Cody and his car.

Not only do we have to spend the weekend together, but we have to drive to Malibu together.

The theme of this nightmare is *together.*

Everything is *together.*

If Chris Evans was my co-star in *The Promised Prince* and I was forced to spend a weekend *together* with him, I wouldn't complain. I'd say, 'Sign me up!' with excitement and vigor. I'm not an unreasonable person. I love a Malibu beach house as much as the next girl.

Just not with Cody Banner.

"Make sure you ask his assistant what flight to Calgary he's booked Cody on, and then find me something different. The last thing I need is to spend the entire weekend with him and then tack on a three-hour flight on top of that. With my luck, we'd be seated next to each other in first class."

"Yes," Winnie says, taking a lot of short little steps to keep up with my long legs. "I've already made a note to get you on a different flight."

"Perfect." I breathe easier.

But my expression sours when I catch a glimpse of Cody up ahead. He's in the same white T-shirt and gray shorts he wore in our meeting with Quinton forty minutes ago. He leans against the side of a golf cart, casually crossing one leg over the other while he talks on the phone.

"He's so handsome." Winnie's words come out reverent, causing me to frown at her. "Oh. Sorry." She shakes her head. "I know we're supposed to hate him."

"I don't *hate* him." I glance at Cody, noticing the easy way he laughs as he talks on the phone. I can admit his genuine smile is cute if you're into straight teeth and perfectly shaped lips that mesh into his beard with sexy charm—which I am into but pretend not to be. "His personality just rubs me the wrong way."

"So this weekend is a big waste of time?"

"No, I'm sure I can find something redeeming about him. I have to if I want my acting career to go beyond this one show."

Cody's gaze shifts to us as we approach. I give a slight smile out of civility. See, I can be mature.

He straightens, looking right at me as he continues his phone conversation. "So you're going topless, huh?" There's a flirty quality behind his smile. "I'm a sucker for topless."

My eye roll is so dramatic it mimics the complete arc of a rainbow.

"All the way naked is my absolute favorite. It's fun when everything hangs in the wind." He wags his brows at me as he speaks.

"Ugh!" I groan. "Can you please tell whatever topless bimbo you're talking to that you'll have to discuss her naked body hanging in the wind later because we need to leave for Malibu?"

Cody's smile hitches upward as if my comment amused him. "See you in a sec." He ends the call with me staring back at him.

"See you in a sec?" I repeat. "Did you invite your topless bimbo friend to Malibu with us?"

He takes a step closer, invading my space with his destructive smile. "Are you nervous you'll have a little competition for my attention?"

"Hardly." I turn my head and avoid eye contact. "I'd rather you be her problem than mine."

"Well, I hate to disappoint you, but"—he points to the black Jeep Wrangler slowing toward us—"that's the topless bimbo you're referring to. She's a beauty, isn't she?"

I study the car, slowly registering my misunderstanding. The doors and roof have all been removed, making it *topless* and *naked*.

"You can apologize for assuming the worst about me."

I hate that I judged him so hard. Usually, I give everyone the benefit of the doubt, but with Cody, I keep creating a narrative around him to convince myself that I'm not attracted to him and definitely shouldn't fall for him.

"Okay, fine. I judged you. But can you blame me? You wanted me to think you were talking to a woman."

An average-sized man in his twenties with a pencil mustache hops out of the car. I've seen him enough times, trailing behind Cody, to know he's his assistant.

"The Jeep is full of gas and ready to hit the road."

I reach my hand out to him. "Hi, I'm Jenna. I don't think we've met yet."

The guy's mouth drops in awe, but he takes my hand.

"Shaking hands seems too formal." I pull him in, air kissing near each of his cheeks. "This is how they do it in Europe, and I love it. It's more personal." I step back, looking expectantly at him.

"This is Julio." Cody chuckles, clapping a hand on his assistant's shoulder. "I think he's a little tongue-tied from meeting the famous Jenna Lewis face to face."

"Oh, you don't have to be nervous." I bounce my shoulders up and down. "I'm just a regular person, like everyone else."

"No, you're not like everyone else." Julio's words come out almost like a whisper.

"Okay. That's enough of that. Thanks, Julio." Cody raises his brows at me. "Are you ready to hit the road?"

I give one more smile to his assistant before flipping my gaze to the *naked* car, imagining what the highway wind will do to my hair, but complaining about it now would just give Cody the upper hand. I'm sure he chose this specific car for our road trip just to see my reaction. I'm not going to give him the satisfaction.

"Almost." I unzip the front pocket of my suitcase and rummage through my bathroom bag until I find a ponytail holder. I gather my long blonde hair, wrap it into a bun on my head, and fasten the elastic around it. "Now, I'm ready."

Cody gets to my bag first, just as I reach for it. My hand lands on top of his, causing our fingers to fumble with each other's for a second until I jerk my arm away.

"I got it." He smirks at me and then easily lifts the luggage into the back of the Jeep.

I glance behind at Winnie, looking for some solace, but instead, she smiles excitedly. Nothing about Cody or this weekend warrants a smile like that.

I reach for the handle inside the car and hoist myself up. Despite being 5'11", it's a climb to get my body in this monster truck of a Jeep. But again, I'm not giving Cody the satisfaction of thinking I'm annoyed. He jumps into the driver's side and puts on his designer sunglasses, elevating his good looks even more.

I let out a breath.

It'll be a long weekend if he's going to look that good the whole time.

He nods to our assistants. "Don't wait up for us."

I barely catch their waves as we pull away.

CODY

IT'S BEEN twenty years since I played the quiet game. As out of practice as I am, I still went the first fifteen minutes of this car ride without talking to Jenna. Loud music has helped, so has the crosswind. But now we're pulling up to a stoplight, and there's no wind to use as a buffer.

From the corner of my eye, I register the gawking teenage girls in the convertible next to us on Jenna's side, pointing and giggling in my direction. I inwardly smile. I'm used to this kind of attention, but it might not be the worst thing in the world for Jenna to see that people actually like me.

"Hey!" the driver calls to us.

Jenna and I both twist our heads in their direction as the girl says something I can't hear her over the music.

I turn the dial on the radio down. "What was that?"

"Aren't you famous?"

I shrug with an appearance of humble modesty. "Yeah, I am. I get that a—"

"I wasn't talking to you." The girl looks right at me before shifting her gaze to Jenna. "I was talking to her."

Jenna laughs while I try not to let my bruised ego show.

"You're a famous supermodel!" the passenger says.

"Oh, my gosh!" the driver squeals. "You're Jenna Lewis. Only, like, the *most* famous supermodel there is."

"You're *sooooo* pretty," the other girl whines with adoration.

"Aww, thanks, girls." Jenna's smile is genuine. "You two are gorgeous as well. I love your outfit." She points to the driver. "And your hair is such an amazing color," she says to the other.

"You are the nicest!" The passenger extends her arm in

front of her, holding her phone out. "Do you care if we get a selfie?"

"Not at all."

We both shift to the camera, smiling, but the girl pauses, looking at me. I think she's finally recognizing that I'm famous too.

"Hey, do you mind leaning back so you're not in our shot?"

Wow.

I've never felt like a bigger idiot than I do now.

"Sure." I press my back against the leather seat, getting out of their picture.

The light turns green, and the girls shout their thanks as they speed off.

Thanks to the turned-down radio, Jenna and I drive in absolute silence for a few seconds until I can't take it any longer.

"Say it."

"I have nothing to say." She stifles her smile.

"Say it."

She shifts in her seat, facing me with an amused expression. "It's killing you that they recognized me—*not you*—and wanted a picture with me—*not you*—isn't it?"

"Pfft. Like I would care about that."

"Karma, baby." Her smile grows. "Now you know how it feels not to be recognized."

"I have sunglasses on." I wiggle the frames before pushing them higher on the bridge of my nose. "They would've recognized me if my sunglasses were off, just like I would've recognized you on the side of the road if you hadn't been wearing sunglasses."

"If you say so." There's way too much satisfaction in Jenna's whole demeanor. Smugness is rippling off her like sound waves, but instead of being irritated by her cockiness, I love it—major turn-on.

"Furthermore"—since when did I start using words like *furthermore?*—"I was farther away than you, so it was easier for those girls to recognize you and not me."

"Sure." She rotates so she sits forward again.

"But it's fine. I'm happy for you that you have adoring fans. Between Julio and now these teenage girls, I just consider myself lucky to even be in your presence."

She laughs, pressing her head against the back of the seat. With her windblown hair and cute laugh, I'm taken aback. Making Jenna Lewis laugh is easily one of the best things I've ever done.

"You should feel lucky to be in my presence," she jokes with a subtle smile. Actually, it's a cute smile. Jenna Lewis has a very cute smile.

And somewhere inside my stomach, butterflies simmer. I might be excited for this weekend after all.

"THE DESTINATION IS ON YOUR RIGHT," the GPS reports fifty-six minutes later.

I follow alongside the brick wall covered in vines until there's a driveway with a gate. Quinton already gave me the code, and after I punch it into the keypad, the bars slowly swing open.

Jenna cranes her neck, looking down the drive for a glimpse of our weekend getaway. I assume the beach house is nice. You don't offer up your home unless you're pretty sure people will like it.

The driveway bends, and a two-story white stucco house comes into view. Palm trees of different heights stand in front with pots of pink and red flowers next to the wood double doors.

I whistle as I park my Jeep in front of the garage. "Not too shabby."

Jenna doesn't answer; she just looks around. Her gaze stops on two electric bikes leaning against the side of the house.

"Maybe we can go for a ride," I offer. Perfect activity if you don't want to talk to the other person. She can peddle in front, and I can follow behind single file. Seems like a great way to spend the afternoon. Not that I don't want to talk to Jenna. I would like to, but I don't know where to begin. We've already spent so much time together with no talking. How do you start being BFFs all of a sudden? Besides, I have nothing worthwhile to say to her. She's classier than me. We're not on the same level.

Her eyes light a little as she looks over the bikes. "I've always wanted to try an electric bike."

"Me too." Jenna's gaze flicks to me as if she can't believe we have something in common. Even she knows we're not entirely on the same level. "Let's get settled inside, and then we can go for a ride."

Reaching into the back of the Jeep, I pull out both of our bags and carry them to the front door, setting them down to punch in the key code. A battery-operated lock unlatches, giving us access to the house.

Jenna steps inside first, spinning in a full circle, taking in the massive beach-front windows and vaulted ceilings. Her eyes trail up the metal stairs to the second floor before she walks to them, taking one at a time.

I follow her with the bags. "You can have first dibs on the bedrooms. I'm a big believer in ladies first and that kind of stuff."

"What a gentleman." She glances over her shoulder at me with another one of her cute smiles.

"I'm glad you noticed."

At the top of the stairs, she peeks her head into what appears to be the master bedroom. A king-sized bed faces a wall of windows that lead out to a large balcony facing the ocean. "I'll take this room." She reaches for her bag. "Thanks." We make the luggage pass off with minimal touching and eye contact.

"I'll just be next door." I keep walking down the hall but stop before escaping into my room. "So, bike ride?"

"Sure, let me just unpack and change my clothes, and I'll meet you downstairs in twenty minutes."

"It's a date."

Jenna's gaze is pointed. "It's *not* a date."

My shoulder presses against the doorframe. "What should we call it, then?"

"How about a bike ride?"

My expression turns sultry. "An *electric* bike ride."

"Nope, just a bike ride." I sense her annoyance as her bedroom door clicks shut.

What do I need to do to get this woman to like me?

I don't know, but I'm not giving up that easily.

CHAPTER
FIVE

JENNA

I DROP my suitcase on my bed and unzip the top, pulling out my clothes one by one.

"Winnie!" I hold up a silky pajama item. Judging by the lingerie, the skimpy swimsuits, and the sexy dresses she included, I can only guess what she thinks—or *hopes*—will happen between Cody and me this weekend. These are the risks you take when you let a hopeless romantic pack for you. Or maybe Tawny got ahold of her. Heaven knows she's hoping for fireworks between me and Cody this weekend.

My best options for a casual Friday afternoon bike ride are a pair of wrap pants and a cropped white tank. Plus, I could use some good fortune, which is exactly what Farida, the street vendor in Bali, promised when I bought the batik wrap pants.

Who doesn't like good fortune?

Or cute pants?

The bright-red geometric fabric looks like a cape for my butt as I use the floor-length mirror to expertly drape it around my legs.

Expertly?

This is my third attempt at magically turning the sheet of

cloth into pants. Attention to detail was needed when Farida demonstrated how to wrap, pull, and tie, but I was so distracted, daydreaming about the good fortune coming my way, that I didn't note the specifics.

I take the fabric in my right hand and fold it over my left hip, slipping the tie through the slit and around my waist. Then I gather the remaining vibrant cloth, pull it up my body, and fold and tuck some more. I'm like those moms who swaddle their babies into a burrito with a single blanket. Finishing off, I tie everything at my waist into a knot, then slowly lift my hands into the air, testing the design and effectiveness of my wrap job. Everything appears secure, but I use a double knot for good measure.

My leg twists as I examine how I look in the mirror. Every angle matters, so I turn, checking my butt from the other side.

Very flattering.

Farida, you genius! I can already *see* the good fortune.

Not that I care how I look. I mean, I do, but not for Cody. More like in case I'm photographed by paparazzi.

I grab a baseball hat and my sunglasses and head downstairs. The front door is open, and Cody is standing on the steps with both bikes behind him, ready to go. A backward baseball cap fits over his head, causing his dark hair to curl over his ears and the back of his neck in the best way. Combine all that dark hair with his short dark beard and piercing blue eyes, and you've got a whole lotta handsomeness.

His gaze pauses on me, and I wonder for a split second if he's appraising me the same way I did him. Most men make it pretty clear every time they look at me what they think of my body or how I look, but Cody is different. When he glances at me, I see nothing but a perfectly masked expression. The girl inside me, the one that's used to men drooling over my looks, feels disappointed by this. But that girl is not in charge here. In fact, she's not in charge anywhere in my life. I fired her when I was twenty-two, right around the same time I realized being pretty wasn't the only thing I wanted to be.

"You ready to go?"

"Yeah." I close the front door behind me. "Do you think there will be a lot of paparazzi out?"

He knocks the kickstand back and holds the bike out to me. "I don't know. I haven't been in this area before."

"I brought these just in case." I place the baseball hat over my hair and put my sunglasses on before taking the bike from him.

"Ah, yes. The lamest disguise ever."

"That didn't stop you from using it."

"Nah"—his toe pushes the kickstand on the other bike—"this is for sun protection."

"You don't even have your hat facing the right way for sun protection."

Cody gives me a knowing smile as we walk down the driveway. "Are you worried people might recognize you with me and think we're dating?"

"No." I shake his words off, but yes. Definitely yes. Hopefully, if paparazzi catch us together, Tawny can play it off as something to do with *The Promised Prince*. But I change the subject to avoid Cody's probing stare. "So, how do you work these things?"

"It's just like riding a bike."

I tilt my head, narrowing my eyes on him and his goofy smirk.

"What? Too vague?"

"Yes."

"Okay, fine." He points to the panel on the handlebars. "Push the plus sign whenever you want more power and the minus sign when you don't."

"Sounds easy enough."

"Should be." The front gate opens after Cody types in the code. "Ladies first—part of the whole gentleman thing we talked about earlier." His hand sweeps out in front of me. "Unless you want me to lead."

"No, I'll go first." I swing my leg over the bike and begin a slow pedal.

"I was hoping you'd say that so I can check out your butt in those pants."

"I heard that," I call over my shoulder. "Some gentleman!"

"Kidding! *Kind of.*" But I hear enough playfulness in his voice to know he is kidding.

I'm actually grateful for Cody's teasing. It breaks the ice just a little bit and helps me relax into an easy rhythm pedaling.

The afternoon sun hits my bare arms, coating them with warmth as an ocean breeze blows my long hair behind me. I breathe in the air, filling my lungs with salt, and for a moment, I'm completely content.

All my problems have vanished.

There's no stress from bad reviews, nerves about filming upcoming scenes, pressure to conjure up chemistry with Cody, or demands to look perfect all the time.

I'm just a girl riding a bike.

I weave through streets, turning to keep us near the shoreline, until we reach the path parallel to the coast. We're going so fast no one has the chance to notice who we really are—another liberating part of the bike ride. And let's not forget about the other best part—the part where I don't have to make forced small talk with Cody.

Eventually, I know we'll have to talk and do what Quinton says, but I like that we're easing into it.

At the boardwalk's end, instead of returning the same way we came, I pull onto the street and try a new route. It's less crowded, with just the occasional passerby or car.

This is pure heaven.

Until it's not.

The end of my heavenly bike ride stops so quickly that I don't even register what's happening until it's too late.

My foot presses against the pedal, but a new tension fights against the movement, making it difficult. I glance down to see what's trapping me as I try to complete another cycle. The bottom of my flowy wrap pants is twirling through the back wheel.

I yank on the fabric, hoping to quickly unhook it before disaster strikes, but there's not enough loose fabric to grab ahold of.

"Stop pedaling!" Cody has obviously noticed my predicament.

But it's too late. The events of the next two seconds have already been put in motion. My legs are forced to a halt as if the pants are some kind of straightjacket for my thighs. The material on my right leg pulls so tight that there's nowhere for it to go but *off* me. There's a loud tearing noise as my wrap pants rip just below the tie at my waist—*freaking double knot!*—leaving me sitting on the bike seat with my bare buttcheeks exposed for the entire world—*and* Cody Banner —to see.

The remaining pant fabric loops through the circling wheel until it pulls taut, stopping the bike. I go to get off, but my pants are wound so tightly between the spokes that I can't move. Without speed forward, I fall to the side, landing on my stomach with the bike on my legs, not even covering my bare butt.

Cody skids to a stop, rushing over. He tears off his sunglasses and bends down so he's eye level with me. I don't know what kind of expression is on my face, but whatever it is, it doesn't portray even half of the embarrassment I feel.

I'm mortified.

Cody is shocked.

And to make everything worse, two men are on the horizon, jogging toward us.

Cody's gaze sweeps over my body, assessing the damage. "Are you hurt?"

I don't answer or move.

I'm frozen—kind of like those girls in horror movies who don't run away right before they're about to be chopped to pieces by an ax murderer, and you keep screaming at the movie, *'Run and hide, you stupid girl! Run and hide!'*

But I'm stuck, so there's no running and hiding. I lie there, clueless about how to solve my indecent-exposure problem. The only thing registering is the airy breeze drifting over my bare skin that wasn't there a few seconds ago...because I had pants on.

Oh, my gosh! I'm not wearing pants!

Cody glances over his shoulder at the two joggers, and suddenly, I'm faced with the reality that more people than just him are witnessing my shame.

He lifts the bike to get it off me and help me to my feet but stops when he notices I'm stuck to the back wheel. He tilts his head back and forth, thinking through how to best help me. "This is unfortunate, isn't it?"

I don't even have time to respond before the joggers are upon us.

"Everything okay here?" I could live a hundred lifetimes and never forget the smirky smile on the good-looking jogger's face as his eyes rove up and down my bare legs and butt.

I turn my head away, pressing my nose against the warm asphalt. The last thing I need is for this stranger to recognize me.

"Yep, we're fine here. I'll take care of this." Cody jumps to his feet, using his body to block me from their stares. He even extends his arms out to the side to cover more width. Like how wide does he think my butt is?

The good-looking jogger flips around as he passes, running backward for a few steps. "Looks like fun. Good luck."

"Thanks." Cody waves at them before turning back to me.

I muster some strength despite my mortification. "I swear, if you make a joke about this, I'll—"

"No jokes." He takes off his white t-shirt and drapes it over my rear end. Is this some kind of smoke-and-mirrors tactic? Is he trying to distract me from my embarrassment with his rippling abs? And, yes, they ripple. Even in my mortified state, lying on my belly, my mind registers the perfect ridges of his six-pack.

A car slowly drives by with its windows down. The passenger's brows dip as she takes us in—me pantless and Cody shirtless. I feel red wash over me like a heat wave in the Mojave Desert.

He crouches beside me, completely unfazed by the onlookers. "Can you move?"

"I don't know."

"So you are hurt?" Concern reaches the edges of his eyes.

"No," I whine. "Just trapped."

His gaze darts to the bike. "Let's see if we can get you to your feet, and then I can try and pull your pants out of the spokes, okay?"

Worst sentence of my life!

I nod, letting him grab under my arms and lift me. I'm able to stand sideways with my hip against the seat. My natural inclination is to spin so my rear is hidden from Cody, but there's not enough leverage or fabric for that, so I settle for holding his t-shirt over my butt with one hand while the other holds the handlebar. But that doesn't do anything to cover the front of me, where my French-cut underwear leaves little to the imagination.

Pretend it's a runway and you're modeling a thong.

Except it's not a runway, and this isn't a controlled photoshoot.

This is real life. *My* real life.

And real-life Jenna Lewis just tore her pants off in front of real-life Cody Banner. How's that for getting to know each other intimately? Thank heavens for laser hair removal.

Cody stands with hands on his hips, studying the back wheel. Even at this high-pressure moment, I'm very aware of his broad shoulders and chiseled chest—I'm aware because my eyes have suddenly turned into Dora the Explorer. If having a perfect body was an Olympic sport, Cody would bring home gold for the United States. How patriotic of him.

"Maybe I can just tear you out of what's left of your pants." He bends down, tugging and pulling. With each yank, my body jerks closer to his head. And I don't even want to think about the *jiggling* that happens to my thighs and butt every time he yanks. I'm hoping his shirt is long enough to hide that.

The horror of the moment is too much, sending my cheeks—face ones, not rear ones (unfortunately, I need to clarify)—blazing with embarrassment once again.

"You know, normally, when I'm shirtless and a woman is pantless, the circumstances are much different." A smile accompanies his words as he tips his gaze up to me. "But I'm not complaining."

"I knew you'd say something like that." I turn my head away from him, not strong enough to meet his gaze while his head is in line with my butt.

"You *knew*?" There's amusement in his voice.

"Yes."

"How?" More wrenching and tugging that seems to lead nowhere.

"Because I'm half naked, and you're a jack—"

"I don't think you're in a position to name-call right now." I glance down just in time to see his playful expression. "Your pants are stuck to a bike."

"You're right." I lift my chin in an attempt at confidence. "Just tear the fabric so we can go home."

"I would if I could." He stands, once again placing his

hands on his hips. "I'm a pretty strong guy"—*yes, we can all see your ridiculously huge biceps*—"but it's going to take more than strength to get your pants out."

"Don't you have, like, a pocketknife or something?"

He pats his six-pack and bare chest. "Does it look like I'm carrying a pocketknife?"

"Well, there has to be some way to extricate me from this nightmare."

"Can you just untie the pants?" His eyes dip to my torso, and I shift my hand, trying to cover myself. That action draws out another one of his amused smiles as his gaze flips back to my eyes. "It's nothing I haven't seen before."

"Still"—my expression is hard—"I'd prefer you *not* see it."

"Okay." He smothers his smirk. "I'll turn around while you untie your pants from your waist."

"Thank you."

I wait until Cody's back is to me before I drape his shirt over the bike and attempt to loosen the knot. But everything is so freaking tight and twisted there's no way to simply untie the pants.

"It's not working."

"Do you want me to try?"

"No!" The last thing I need is Cody's fingers brushing against my stomach.

"So you're stuck?"

"Yes, I'm stuck," I snap.

He flips around, and the huge smile on his face is too much. He's fighting laughter, but I can see his lips and shoulders twitching.

"It's not funny!"

A chuckle puffs out, and he covers his mouth with his hand.

"Stop! It's not funny." But against my will, I laugh too. "Fine. It's a little funny."

We spend the next ten seconds laughing because this is by far the weirdest thing that has ever happened to me.

So much for not ever letting Cody Banner see my vulnerability.

"Okay." He pulls it together. "Let's find someone to help us."

"No! No more people."

"It's fine. This sort of thing always happened to me when I was a kid."

I give him a pointed stare. "Your pants *always* got stuck in the tire spokes?"

"No, it was my shoelaces, but same thing."

"Shoelaces and pants are *not* the same thing."

Ignoring me, he walks down the road, looking into yards for someone to help.

Farida was *so* wrong.

Nothing about these pants brings good fortune.

Worst fortune ever!

Up ahead, Cody flags down a car. I can't hear what he says to the man driving, but there's a lot of pointing at me and smiling, which sucks. The driver hands him something, and Cody jogs to me as the car pulls over.

My eyes swing to the ground, where my hat and sunglasses fell off when I crashed. Right about now, I wish I could hide behind them.

"I have the answer!" Cody waves a lighter in front of me as he approaches.

"A lighter, really?"

"Do you have a better idea?"

Yes, death. Quick and painless so I won't have to relive this moment ever again.

Cody falls to one knee. I hear the crack of the lighter and the smell of smoke as the flame engulfs the cheap fabric from Bali.

"How will you keep the flames from spreading to me?"

It only takes a few seconds before the tension releases, and I'm free.

Hallelujah!

He uses his hands to clap out the rest of the burning fire on the fabric attached to me. Very effective.

Cody returns the lighter to the watching car while I wrap and tuck the remaining pant shreds over me. It looks like a charred fringe mini-skirt—emphasis on *mini*—but it's better than nothing. I pinch the sleeves of Cody's t-shirt into the spaghetti string on the sides of my underwear so his shirt hangs down and covers my backside.

"Ready to get out of here?" he asks when he returns.

"More than ready." I swing my leg over my bike and try to pedal, but it's jammed from the pants, still looped through the rungs. "You've got to be kidding me!"

"No worries." Cody is by my side instantly, taking the bike from me. "I'll just carry it."

"You're going to carry the bike all the way home?"

"Yep." He effortlessly lifts it in front of his body like a dumbbell and walks toward the beach house. "You can ride my bike. I'll meet you there."

For the first time in five months, I don't hate Cody Banner. I'm grateful for him. My smile slips as I watch him and his stupid back muscles trudge ahead.

CHAPTER
SIX

CODY

WHEN I RETURN to the beach house, I'm drenched in sweat and ready for a shower. Jenna is nowhere to be found. No surprise there.

I run up the stairs, passing her closed bedroom door. I'm guessing I won't see her for the rest of the weekend. She'll probably hide just to avoid me and the embarrassment.

She doesn't know that the incident with the bike made her more likable than anything else she's done since I met her. For the first time, she appeared human. All the flawlessness she normally exudes vanished, and I didn't feel intimidated by her. She was vulnerable, and I could finally relate to her. Not the getting-her-pants-ripped-off part, but the part where she wasn't perfect. Okay, she *looked* pretty darn perfect—I might have glanced—but her situation was far from perfect.

After a shower and a change of clothes, I find Jenna on the living room couch with seven cartons of food spread out on the coffee table in front of her. She decided not to hide from me the rest of the weekend after all.

She's in silk baby-blue pajama shorts and a matching spaghetti strap silk top. It's a little early for bedtime apparel, but I'm not complaining since the casualness makes her seem more approachable. And she looks outstanding. I'm not trying to notice how beautiful she is. It just happens.

"I didn't know what you wanted." Her eyes move to me as I come down the stairs. "But I figured you were just as hungry as I am, so I ordered the entire Thai menu."

"Yeah, I'm starving. Thanks." I almost smile, thinking about how difficult it probably was for her to do something nice for me. Instead of sitting, I walk to the kitchen. "What are you drinking?"

She lifts a metal water bottle. "I'm all set."

The refrigerator has little to offer, so I fill a glass of ice water.

"Did you get the bike back okay?"

"I did." I sit down on the other end of the couch, glancing over the food. "You'll be happy to know it isn't broken. I used some of Quinton's tools and got the rest of your pants out of the wheel. I threw the remains in the garbage, but I can easily pull them out if you still want them."

She shakes her head. "I never want to see those pants again."

Settling on a Thai curry, I lean back into the cushion. "I liked the pants. I just liked them better when they were off you."

Jenna's leg kicks out like a ninja, shoving the side of my thigh with her foot. "I thought you weren't going to joke about this."

"I'm not joking." I grab her bare ankle, stopping her kicks. "I did like them better off of you."

She pulls her leg back out of my touch. "I'm never riding a bike again."

"Oh, come on. It wasn't that bad."

"It was." She chooses a carton of fried rice and relaxes in her spot. "Thank you for helping me. You didn't have to do that, but I appreciate it."

"Do you really think I would've left you stuck to the bike?"

"I haven't always been the most cordial person to work with, so I wouldn't blame you for leaving me to fend for myself. But you were cool about it, even giving me your shirt. I just didn't expect that, you know?"

So basically, she thought I'd make fun of her and then leave her alone to die. Jenna's opinion of me is worse than I thought. We eat in silence for a solid two minutes because what do you talk about with a person who thinks so little of you? Besides, even if she thought I had some redeeming qualities, we have nothing in common to help strike up a conversation.

She must feel it too, because she blurts, "I thought we could play twenty questions while we eat." My chewing pauses, and I look back at her. "You know, to get to know each other a little more in case Quinton quizzes us or something stupid like that."

I swallow, nodding a little too emphatically. "Sure. If you want."

That reaction causes Jenna to doubt herself. "Never mind. It's a stupid idea."

"No, it's not stupid. Quinton probably will quiz us when we get back."

Her mouth moves into a hesitant smile. "So you want to?"

I mean, do I *want* to answer personal questions about myself? No, I do not. But I also don't want to make Jenna feel bad or for news to get back to Quinton that I wasn't trying this weekend.

"Yeah, let's do it." I'm not sure what the appropriate amount of enthusiasm is for a grown man in this type of situation, but I'm pretty sure I missed the mark by a long shot. "Do we just start with the basics? Like, what's your favorite color?"

She grabs her phone off the coffee table and swipes through a few screens. "I already looked up some questions online."

"Oh, okay." I guess we really are doing this.

Her body straightens as she reads off the first question. "What's your favorite part of the day and why?"

"Dusk."

She blinks at me. "Dusk?"

"It's peaceful. What's yours?"

"Sunrise." She smiles. "Because it's peaceful."

"Dusk is more peaceful."

"We can agree to disagree." Her smile widens as her eyes drop to her phone again. "What's the latest I can call you at night, and you'd still pick up?"

"Midnight. Maybe one in the morning."

"I guess that makes sense with your lifestyle."

"My lifestyle? Are you implying that I'm out partying every night?"

"Are you?"

"No." But I can see from the flash in her eyes that she doesn't believe me.

"Well, the latest you can call me is ten o'clock."

"Not surprising."

"Are you implying that I'm boring?"

"Are you boring?"

"No, I just like to get a full night's sleep." Jenna's gaze swings from me to her phone, finding her next question. "How did you decide what you wanted to do for a living?"

"I didn't decide. I moved to LA when I was eighteen. Worked at a Gold's Gym until a talent agent approached me and invited me to be in my first movie. Everything just took off from there."

Her brows pinch. "You didn't have a plan?"

Yeah, I planned to move as far away as possible from my parents. I was finally an adult, out of their reach, out of their manipulation games, and out of their ability to claim me as a tax dependent. I fulfilled my plan. Everything after that was just gravy, but I don't tell people that stuff, let alone a woman who hates me.

"Nope, no plan."

She nods, comparing my answer to the one in her head that I know she's about to tell me. "Our plan was winning pageants and building a modeling career. When I was eight, I started competing in pageants and did some modeling jobs for local boutiques. By the time I was twelve, I'd done a few campaigns for Gap and Old Navy. But things took off after winning Miss Teen USA and landing my first Coca-Cola commercial. That's what opened the door for my career. It was everything we'd been working for."

"We?"

"My mom and me."

"So being a model was your mom's dream?"

"No. We both decided on that plan."

I can't help my eye roll.

"What?"

"You were eight. You should've been playing Barbies, not running around to pageants and modeling calls."

"I played with Barbies."

"That's not the point. Your mom used you to carry out her dreams and live vicariously through your success." I gesture to her. "You're lucky you had the genes, and everything worked out. But for most kids, it doesn't end with a multimillion-dollar modeling career. They're the pawn in their parents' games until they don't benefit them anymore, and they cast them aside."

Jenna leans her arm against the back of the couch. "Is that what happened to you?"

"No." I puff out a rough laugh. "We're talking about you." But just in case I was projecting my own pathetic story into our conversation, I stand and carry a few cartons of food to the refrigerator so Jenna can't read the expression on my face.

"Fine. Next question. Tell me about your parents."

I glance over my shoulder at her. "That's not on your list."

"How do you know?"

"Because it doesn't go from *How late can I call you?* to *Tell me about your screwed-up parents.*"

"Are your parents screwed up?" Her eyes follow me as I make my way back to the couch.

"Whose aren't?" I say, taking a seat again.

"That's a really pessimistic thought."

"I guess I'm a pessimistic person."

"But you're not. You never take anything seriously and make inappropriate jokes when you're uncomfortable or don't know how to respond." And Quinton claims Jenna doesn't know anything about me. "So why don't you take this question seriously and tell me about your parents?"

"There's not a lot to tell." I blow out a breath. "They both worked a lot. I'm an only child, so I spent most of my childhood alone. When I was nine, they decided to split, and then they spent the next seven years in a custody battle fighting over me."

"A seven-year custody battle? Is that even possible?"

"It is when you have good lawyers and money to drag out the conflict."

"I guess that's good that they both wanted you."

"They didn't want me. They just wanted to use me to hurt each other."

"How did that make you feel?"

I've never been to therapy—probably should've—but I imagine it feels a lot like this.

"Like a pawn." I'm surprised by my honest answer. I'm never honest about my past. "When I was sixteen, custody was awarded to my mom, but by the time I was seventeen, she took off with a new guy."

"What do you mean *took off?*"

"Like, left. I came home from school one day, and she wasn't there."

"Did you try calling her?"

"Nope. I had all this freedom and no responsibility. I wasn't going to ruin that by calling her."

"Did you go and live with your dad then?"

"Nope. I never told him she was gone."

"How did you survive? What about food and house payments?"

"I lived off the child support checks from my dad that were automatically deposited into my bank account until I graduated high school."

"What about school?"

"I went to school…enough to graduate."

"Didn't anyone check on you? A principal or a teacher?" The disbelief in Jenna's eyes is apparent. I'm used to that kind of reaction, honestly. It's typical when you tell people your mom abandoned you during some of your most impressionable teenage years.

"People probably should've checked on me." I shake my head. "But no one did."

Pity fills the edges of her gaze. "So, were you miserable and lonely?"

"Nah. I was living the ultimate teenage-boy fantasy. My house was the bachelor pad, and I took full advantage of it." I smile, shielding her from my real feelings. I was lonely, *very* lonely. Mostly at night, when all my friends went home to their families. That was when I started inviting girls over. I just wanted someone to fill the silence, even if it was just them breathing while they slept next to me.

Jenna nods in a that-explains-a-lot-about-you kind of way. And for reasons I don't understand, I'm dying to know if the pity in her eyes is real, if she'll take pity and stop judging me for everything she thinks I am and start seeing me for all the things I could be.

73

"That's really sad, Cody." She smiles in one of those sad kinds of ways. "I'm sorry that happened to you."

"Eh, it was a long time ago." I hold her stare, trying to convey that I genuinely appreciate it, but every tender moment of vulnerability has to stop somewhere, so I clap, startling Jenna, and carefully put my masked facade back in place. "But it's fine. My dysfunctional teenage years led to bigger and better things." I casually lean into the cushion. "What about you? Are your parents screwed up too?"

Jenna frowns. "I still have so many questions about your upbringing, but I'll save them for another time and switch to me out of fairness." She brushes her hair back from her face as she thinks. "I wouldn't say my parents are screwed up. My dad is a little difficult. Everything is his way or the highway, but it hasn't been a big problem in our family. We just know how he is." Meaning everyone just passively lets him get away with being a jerk—I can read between the lines well enough. "He's a little hard on my brother with all the sports stuff. You know, demands a lot of perfection from him."

"But not you?"

"I'm his baby girl." She shrugs innocently. "It's not the same. I'm already perfect in his eyes."

"And your mom?"

"He's not the nicest to her, but deep down, I know he loves her."

"I meant, what's your relationship like with your mom?"

"Oh." A spark of embarrassment flits across her face. "I guess there's some truth to what you said earlier. My mom's goals became my goals. She probably did live vicariously through me. Pushed her ideals onto me. From a young age, I knew I always had to look my best. It wasn't ladylike to show flaws. But in her defense, I think my father demands perfection from her. It's all she's known, so she taught it to me."

This insight into Jenna's family explains a lot about her and the way I've perceived her on set—the overanalyzing of each scene and the need for detailed explanations. It's all so she can appear perfect and not show any weakness.

"Okay, next question." She abruptly changes the subject without warning. I guess it's a little hard for everyone to take a subjective look into their family and past. Her eyes whip to me. "Would you spontaneously take a trip with someone you just met?"

"Isn't that what we're doing here?"

"No." She laughs, and I'm glad to see her pure joy again. "We didn't just meet. We just don't like each other."

I twist my body, facing her more. "No, you decided you didn't like me from day one."

"And what? You wanted to be best friends as soon as we met?"

"Why not?"

Jenna's smile fades, and she looks away. "We're too different."

"Opposites attract."

"Not in this case."

Her resolve to dislike me stirs up a determination to win her approval.

She picks up her phone again. "Blonde, brunette, or redhead?" Her eyes bounce to me with a warning. "And don't say all three."

I hold her stare. "Blonde."

And that's not even a line. I've always been a sucker for tall blondes, exactly like the woman sitting one cushion apart from me.

"I bet." She blows my answer off, glancing at the list. "What was your first kiss like?"

"Sloppy."

"Mine too." She laughs. "What was your *best* kiss like?"

"Every kiss is the best kiss." Jenna rolls her eyes at my remark. "And you? What was your best kiss like?"

She answers without hesitation. "I'm still waiting for it."

"I would've thought a woman like you would've been thoroughly kissed by now."

"Oh, I've been thoroughly kissed by a long line of men who only wanted to date me because I'm a model or because being with me would help their career or elevate their status. But I'm still waiting for a life-changing kiss from a man who loves me for me. That'll be the difference maker."

"So you've never been in love or in a serious relationship?"

"No." She inclines her head, assessing me. "Have you?"

"I'm not built for love and relationships, a consequence of my bachelor teenage years. I'm pre-wired for a life of singlehood."

"That's stupid. Everyone is built for love. It's a basic human emotion."

"Okay, fine. Love maybe. But marriage isn't happening. I'll be an eternal bachelor."

"Why? Because of how your parents' marriage ended up?"

"I've just seen too much of the dark side. Maybe things would've been different if my parents had been different, but those were the cards I was dealt, and this is how I'm playing them."

"You don't have to repeat your parents' relationship. You can stop the cycle, you know?"

"Staying single *is* me stopping the cycle."

"If that's really the life you want, you're doing a good job living it."

Jenna's words feel like a put-down, mainly because I'd just opened up to her and thought she understood. But I guess it's too much to ask for somebody like her to understand. She's got the perfect all-American family behind her, shaping her ideals about love and relationships.

"I'm guessing you want to get married."

Her shoulders drop in a daydream sort of way. "More than anything."

"Why?" I try to keep the judgment out of my voice, but I don't think I'm successful.

"Life is about experiences, and I want to share those experiences with someone I love."

"Why not just share them with a friend?"

Her nose scrunches as she shakes her head. "It's not the same. Marriage provides a bond stronger than anything else. When two people are mentally, physically, and emotionally on the same page, no other relationship can beat it."

"But what happens when they're no longer on the same page?"

"You keep working at it until your marriage gets back to where it needs to be."

"Or you drag your only son through a seven-year custody battle."

"Not every marriage has to be like that. If you want something different, you can make it what you want or need."

"Yeah, maybe." I rub my eyes, tired of how emotionally draining this conversation is. I decide to switch to a question that's not about me or love or marriage. "Why did you decide to change from modeling to acting?"

She flicks an imagined speck of dust off her thigh. "I'm twenty-six years old. I *maybe* have five to eight good years left modeling before younger up-and-coming women will replace me, and that's if I don't completely blow up my career by becoming a mom, which I want to become. But if I transition from modeling to acting, I can work and stay relevant longer."

Her response is a little rehearsed, and her smile lacks genuineness, making me think there's more behind her decision than she's letting on, but I don't press for the rest of the story because her rehearsed answer sounds a lot like my reasons for trying to restore my image. We're both setting ourselves up for our future.

We just might have more in common than either of us thinks.

"Sounds like you have your career all figured out," I say.

"Not if *The Promised Prince* doesn't do well." Jenna's eyes drop to her lap. "There's a lot on the line for me."

I hadn't thought about how a failed series would affect her. I'd only thought about it from my standpoint—it would be embarrassing, but I'd be able to bounce back from the negativity and find work again as long as I prove to fans that I'm growing up and maturing. But if *The Promised Prince* flops, it could mean the end of Jenna's acting career before it even begins.

"So we'll turn the narrative around," I offer, and surprisingly, my voice is upbeat and hopeful. I'm not sure I've ever heard this kind of tone from myself.

Her green eyes lift. "How are we going to turn it around?"

"Let's go over a few scenes tomorrow, choreograph some movement and physicality into them."

"I thought you hated blocking and spelling everything out." Her voice changes as if she's imitating something I've said. "You just want us to act."

"Yes, that's typically how I roll, but nothing is typical about our situation. I've never *not* had on-screen chemistry with a costar."

"So I'm the problem?"

"I don't know what the problem is." I shake my head. "I just know we were sent to Malibu to fix it, and for the sake of our reputations in the industry, we can't show up Monday without some improvement."

"So instead of getting to know each other, you want to practice our lines and add physical touch to them?"

"Sort of. I want to get to know you physically. Build chemistry that way."

There's uncertainty in Jenna's eyes, a hesitation that reminds me why I can't get comfortable around her in the first place. It's hard to create chemistry with a person when all they see are the worst parts of you.

"Okay," she finally agrees. "It's worth a try."

"Tomorrow, then?"

"Tomorrow."

I don't think I've ever been more excited or nervous for an acting class in my entire life.

CHAPTER
SEVEN

JENNA

SO MANY WORDS drift through my mind, making it impossible to fall asleep. Words said earlier tonight. Twenty questions with Cody was dangerous. Now I want twenty more. And after that, I'm betting I'll want another twenty and another.

I scratched the surface of who Cody Banner is, but already, I'm learning so much about why he's the way he is and what shaped him to be this way. But that's what makes this game so dangerous. What if the more I learn, the more allowances I make for his playboy behavior until I completely disregard all my reasons for keeping him at bay and end up falling for him?

That's a pretty specific domino effect, but that's what I'm scared of. A logical fear for a girl like me. I've always been a sucker for a charming-bad-boy persona. I blame it on thirteen-year-old Jenna and her obsession with Danny Zuko from *Grease*. But I'm not thirteen anymore. I'm twenty-six, and I'm done dating emotionally unavailable guys whose flex is how many supermodels they've been with. I vowed I wouldn't do it anymore, and if you don't take a vow seriously, what kind of personal integrity do you even have?

So my walls are up, and even with the walls around my heart, I placed a warden to stand guard for extra protection. Ain't nobody getting through—especially Cody.

Not that Cody's goal is to hook up with me. But I'd be stupid to ignore the facts. He's notorious for dating his costars, and I refuse to be the next woman who can't resist Hollywood's biggest playboy. I'm here for longevity, for respect, for a career that I can count on for the next two decades, and starting a relationship during my first show as a new actress isn't a good look, no matter how soft his soft side is.

That's why I'm currently freaking out.

Cody said, and I quote, "I want to get to know you physically." Like, what the heck am I supposed to do with that? How am I supposed to play along with this *let's build physical chemistry* game while also guarding my heart? Trying to figure all that out has me staring at the ceiling in the dark at 11:36 p.m.

But then my phone lights everything up.

Tawny: What exactly happened in Malibu today?

Tawny knows what happened. The first thing I did when I returned from the bike ride was text Tawny and tell her about my mortifying experience.

Jenna: Nothing happened besides my pants being taken off me.

I frown at how bad that sounds.

Tawny: Well, look what just popped up on my feed.

I click the link she sent, and suddenly, my screen fills with a picture of Cody carrying my bike—*shirtless*. Black, bold letters at the top of the article read: '**Who's the Mystery Woman that Went Home with Cody Banner's Shirt as a Souvenir?**'

I gasp as my eyes quickly scan the second picture. It's of me riding away, but the back of me. Thankfully, Cody's shirt covers my butt. I read through the article as fast as I can, looking for any sign of my name, but it's all about how Cody started his bike ride in Malibu wearing a shirt—there's even a picture for added proof—and then ended up giving it to a mysterious woman. The author of the article draws only one conclusion: Cody must've paused his bike ride to fool around with a woman who then kept his shirt as a souvenir because that's the *only* logical reason why he's shirtless. The most ridiculous part is that the article doesn't even touch on the fact that he's carrying the bike instead of riding it.

My eyes drift to the white t-shirt draped across the back of the chair in my room.

I'm the mystery woman who went home with Cody Banner's shirt.

Tawny: Are you sure you didn't leave out any details?

Jenna: I guess I left out the part where he gave me his t-shirt to help cover me up.

Tawny: You came home pantless, and he came home shirtless. I want to know what happened after you both were half-naked.

Jenna: Oh, my gosh! NOTHING HAPPENED.

Tawny: That's really a shame. Sounds like a wasted opportunity between two people who are trying to create chemistry.

I roll my eyes as I click the link to the article again and read through the words slowly. Cody's reputation as a playboy is the clear message of the story. If I had come across the article on my own, I would've believed every single implication, but since I lived this moment in real life, I'm very aware of the inaccuracies.

The corner of my mouth lifts. Cody took his shirt off in public so that I didn't have to walk around with my butt exposed, and because of it, his reputation took a hit. Talk about taking one for the team in a very sweet way.

But just because he gave me the shirt off his back—literally—doesn't mean I'm charmed by him. Even he admitted that he's only interested in being a bachelor for the rest of his life. If that's not the definition of a true playboy, then I don't know what is. And I'm done being the most recent flavor of the month for men like that.

I'm looking for longevity, marriage, children, grandchildren, and the entire happily-ever-after package. Cody Banner is definitely not a guy headed there.

Another text appears at the top of my screen, causing me to gasp...*again*. If anyone else were here, they'd think my lung was punctured with all this gasping for air, but I can't help it. It's like my thoughts summoned Cody Banner.

Unknown Number: Hey, Jenna. This is Cody.

Note to my beating heart: you are a traitor. Where's the heart warden when I need him?

I switch back to Tawny's message.

Jenna: You're not going to believe it. Cody just texted me.

Tawny: Wait. Aren't you with him at Quinton's beach house?

Jenna: Yes, but I'm in my bedroom, and he's in his.

Tawny: What did he say? Is he inviting you to join him?

Jenna: No! Just 'hey' and that it was him. Wait. Another text came through. Let me read it.

I swipe to his thread.

Unknown Number: I know it's after 10 p.m., and that's your cutoff, but I can't sleep. I thought about looking over the script to prepare for tomorrow, but I didn't bring mine. Do you have a copy I can borrow?

I take a screenshot of his text and send it to Tawny.

Tawny: Ugh! Are you two working? No wonder you guys have no chemistry. You're the most boring sexy couple I've ever seen.

Jenna: We're reviewing our scenes to see how we can add physical touch to them. He wants to get to know me physically.

Tawny: Now that's what I want to hear. You should've led with that.

Another text from Cody pops up, and I switch over.

Unknown Number: Maybe you're already asleep. If you get this when you wake up, no worries.

My fingers quickly slide over my keyboard. For some

reason, I don't want the conversation to end with him just thinking I'm asleep.

Jenna: I'm awake.
Jenna: I have a copy of the script you can borrow.

Unknown Number: Only if you're not using it.

Jenna: No, I won't look at it until tomorrow morning.

Unknown Number: Okay, can I come grab it?

Jenna: Yeah, just give me one second.

I leap out of bed like one of those track-and-field hurdle jumpers and glance in the mirror. There's enough moonlight coming in from the balcony for me to make sure I still look decent. Whoa, whoa, whoa. Why do I even care how I look in front of him? I don't. I tousle my hair just to prove to myself that I can be ugly and not care.

My phone lights again, and I pick it up.

Tawny: I zoomed into his picture in the article. After seeing his chest and muscles, please tell me exploring the ridges of his pecs and six-pack is part of your practice tomorrow.

I shake my head.

Jenna: Can you stay focused? Any physical touch that happens tomorrow is about building on-screen chemistry. It has nothing to do with how attractive Cody or his abs are.

Tawny: So you admit to finding him attractive?

Jenna: You're a terrible friend. Do you know that?

Tawny: And you avoided answering my question. Come on. Spill the beans.

Jenna: I avoided answering the question because whether or not I find Cody Banner attractive is a non-issue. We work together, and that's the only relationship we'll ever have.

Tawny: Not true. For you to have on-screen chemistry with this man, you need to find him attractive off-screen, which shouldn't be hard.

Unknown Number: Okay, be there in a sec.

Cody's newest text slides onto the top of my screen. What is with the intense heartbeats happening in my chest right now? I drop brick by brick on each beat, hoping my fortifying wall can smother them out.

Tawny: Do you get what I'm saying about the need to find this man attractive for your career?

Holy cow, Tawny. I cannot deal with you right now and keep my thoughts and feelings in the appropriate box. Cody Banner is about to stop by my bedroom for a clandestine meeting. Actually, there's nothing clandestine about borrowing my script, but I'm panicking regardless, and I don't even know why.

I tell Tawny what she wants to hear to get her off my back, pushing send on the text.

Jenna: Fine. I can admit that Cody Banner has the most exquisite chest, arms, and six-pack I've ever seen. I don't need to zoom into the picture to know that. I witnessed it firsthand. And I can also admit that, yes, I find his arrogant, bad-boy persona attractive sometimes. Now, if we knew whether or not he was a good kisser in real life, that may impact if we have any chemistry *winky-face emoji*

There's a knock on my door, and I grab *The Promised Prince* script before opening it.

"Hey!" Why do I sound so winded? It was a four-foot walk.

The hallway light illuminates Cody's bare chest and arms. Does this man ever wear a shirt? From a peripheral angle, I see his cotton shorts slung low on his waist, and my brain starts yelling at my eyes, TAKE A BETTER LOOK! FOR THE LOVE, WOMAN! TAKE A BETTER LOOK! But I stay strong, holding eye contact like my life depends on it.

"Hey." He smiles in return.

There's a text alert, and he lifts his hand, glancing at his phone. I don't even mind when he completely ignores me to read the text because now I can indulge my eyes.

And what an indulgence!

Tan skin.

Effortless, defined stomach muscles.

And two perfectly edged out Vs trailing down his hips. Thank goodness cotton shorts don't have belt loops. Otherwise, I might not have seen those Vs.

Cody snickers, and my eyes whip to his face.

A smirky smile covers his mouth. "The most exquisite chest, arms, and six-pack you've ever seen?"

He caught me staring. I'm lame. So very lame.

Wait.

My heart hammers as I blink at him and his way-too-satisfied smile.

Those words sound awfully familiar.

Cody holds his phone screen in front of me. The text meant for Tawny glares back at me like my own personal scarlet letter of humiliation.

I sent the text to him?

I sent the text to him!

My mouth falls open, but no sound comes out.

His smile goes from smirky to swaggering in the blink of an eye. "I *am* a good kisser in real life. If you want to practice that tomorrow, we can."

What short-term-memory superpower allows him to already have the entire text memorized by heart?

"Ha!" I cackle, finally snapping out of stunned silence. "I was just joking with you."

That smile of his is bigger than anything I've ever seen. "Are you sure?"

He's on to me.

I hate him for it.

I will deny this to my grave.

"Mm-hmm. I'm sure." I nod, but the way Cody leans toward me and how his smile hitches at the corner tells me he's not buying what I'm selling. "Fine." My shoulders drop. So much for denying this to my grave. "I meant to send that text to Tawny. She kept harassing me about whether or not we're finding chemistry here. So I said all of that to get her off my back."

"To get her off your back?" It's his turn to nod. "So you didn't mean it?"

"Didn't mean it."

"Okay."

He stares at me, and it's like he's looking into my soul. Is this some kind of chemistry-building exercise? The first to blink fails? I purposely blink because, despite it all, I'm still in control here.

His brows lift. "The script?"

"Right." My arm shoots up, waving it in front of him. "Here you go."

Slowly, his fingers brush over mine as he retrieves it from my hand. He must live by the motto *the slower, the better* because it seems like Cody has only one gear, and it's called sexy-slow.

"Thanks." He takes one step like he's leaving but stops, overcorrecting into my space. "By the way…" His voice is husky and low, building off-the-charts tension in my chest. "I think you're a beautiful woman, and I'm attracted to you too."

Those words flatline me. I'm dead. Just order the casket now.

"It's only fair that you know—just to even the score." He takes a step back. "Goodnight, Jenna. I'll see you tomorrow."

"Goodnight." I incline my head, watching him walk down the hall to his room. Dang, those sexy back muscles. They get me every time.

I close my door, sliding down it until I'm a puddle on the floor.

There's no chance of sleep now.

Somehow, I lost control of the conversation.

Where was my freaking heart warden on that one?

CHAPTER
EIGHT

CODY

JULIO PACKED COLOGNE.

The good kind that makes me effortlessly smell like a mixture of soap and deodorant, so it seems like I'm *not* wearing cologne—which is what I'm going for. The last thing I need is for Jenna Lewis to think I put cologne on for her, even though I did, but I don't want her to know that. I just want her to think I naturally smell this good. It's hard to follow, even for me.

My fingers run over my cheeks, patting my beard down as I glance at myself in the living room mirror.

I look good.

We've already established I smell good.

My breath is the last thing to check.

I cup my hands in front of my mouth, pushing out a puff of air and quickly sniffing it. Minty fresh.

Not that Jenna and I are going to kiss.

I mean, we *could* kiss.

We're getting to know each other physically today, so I suppose a kiss is on the table.

The thought drop-kicks my stomach, sending it flying through the air.

If Quinton had told me yesterday morning that I'd have to kiss Jenna this weekend, I would've balked at the idea. But something shifted yesterday. Could've been the disastrous bike ride, the twenty questions, or her accidental text last night. Who knows?

Okay, I know.

It was the accidental text.

I've only read through it a hundred times. I even took the liberty of screen-shotting it so she couldn't see the little dots dance on her end. I'm smart like that.

Never underestimate the power of a woman complimenting your physique. Those accidental five sentences give me more confidence than my entire dating history ever has.

Jenna Lewis finds me attractive.

This changes everything.

I can finally stop worrying that every time I touch her, she'll gag, or cringe, or worse, break into hives (this new information gives me hope that the hives weren't entirely my fault).

Quinton wants chemistry, and that's what he's going to get.

"Are you ready?" Jenna asks as she comes down the stairs, holding her script.

I saw her earlier this morning when she came downstairs to use the gym on the main floor, but now she's changed into jean shorts and a cropped shirt with a scoop neck that's fallen off one shoulder in the sexiest way possible, giving me the perfect look at the string bikini straps tied around her neck.

She points outside. "I thought we could do this by the pool. Maybe it will help us feel like we're actually on vacation."

"Sure." I nod, gesturing for Jenna to lead the way. She sits on the edge of a lounge chair with the script on her knees.

"Do you have a plan or a specific scene you want to start with?"

"I thought we could go over the dancing scene first. It's the first time in a long time that Trev and Renna actually touch, and it's a pivotal moment leading into the kiss."

"That's true." She looks down and begins flipping through the pages to find the scene.

I extend my arm, putting my hand above the script, right in her line of sight. Jenna's head slowly lifts.

"Dance with me."

She looks around nervously. "Right now?"

"Why not? It's in the scene."

"Don't you want to go over our lines first and all the spacing that leads up to the actual dance?"

The crack of a grin spreads across my lips. "When have I ever wanted to go over spacing?"

Jenna frowns. "Never."

"Right. So why would I want to go over it now?"

"I guess you wouldn't."

"Besides, we know the lines. Now, we need to know each other, how our bodies react to touch, and how we move in the space together. That's when real chemistry can build." I wiggle my fingers in front of her. "So dance with me."

"I just didn't know we were starting so soon. I thought we'd ease into the touching."

"Relax, it's just a dance."

Her green eyes drop to my proffered hand, then back to me. "You're right. It's just a dance."

Jenna slips her hand into mine, letting me pull her to her feet. An outbreak of warmth spreads through my fingers, spiking sensitivity in each nerve ending.

"How do you like to be held?"

"We should probably look and see how the script says the scene should go."

"No." I shake my head, gently tugging her body closer to mine. "How do *you* like to be held?"

Jenna's body stills as I release her hand and slip my fingers around her bare waist. I can thank her cropped shirt for the skin-to-skin contact. My touch is soft and feathery, hesitant until commanded to do more.

"I don't know what you mean."

"Yes, you do." I incline my head, tracing the tip of my nose along her cheek, neck, ear, and bare shoulder without ever touching her with more than my breath.

She tilts her head, increasing the width of her skin I can access. "What are you doing?"

"Memorizing how you feel."

Her breaths are sharp and ragged. "Besides your hand on my back, you aren't even touching me."

"I can still *feel* you." In the way my heart is hammering, in how she smells, in the small shudder of her shoulder, the warmth radiating from her waist, and the goosebumps traveling down her arm. The space between us melts away as my body reacts to her body, building a template of physical chemistry one square inch at a time.

"So, how do you like to be held?"

"I...I...don't know."

Loose strands of her hair tickle my lips as I speak into her ear. "Do you like a firm grip around your waist? Do you like a soft palm on your back? Do you like full body contact? Or space between the hips with arms doing all the work?"

"I've never thought about it before."

"Yes, you have." My lips graze the shell of her ear.

Her chest rises and falls until she finally says, "I like a strong hand at my waist and full body contact."

"See?" Firmly cupping my right hand around her, I scoot her hips and chest into mine. "That wasn't so difficult, was it?"

Hesitantly, she wraps one arm around my back, pressing

her palm against my shoulder blade. The excitement of Jenna's body next to mine is like riding the front row on a roller coaster, anticipating the twists, turns, and drops ahead. Uncertainty and exhilaration accompany each breath.

"Do you like spins and turns when you dance or slow rocking?" My other hand trails the length of her free arm until it closes over her fingers. I lift our joined hands, holding them in the air beside us.

"It depends on the guy." She pulls her head back, eyeing me from the side. "If I'm not interested in him, I'd rather have spins and turns instead of the intimacy of slow rocking."

"What about with me?" I keep her gaze.

"We could slowly move back and forth." Her eyes drift away from mine as her shoulders lift in a shrug. "That would be best for the show."

"This isn't about the show. Not really." My weight shifts back and forth as I hug her body into mine. "This is about you and me and building a physical relationship between us."

"Okay." Her chest rises against mine as her grasp around my back tightens.

I don't say anything more. Just slowly rock us back and forth to the music of the crashing waves in the distance. Our joined hands relax and casually rest against my chest, where my heart is beating steadily.

There's still a stiffness to Jenna, like she can't fully allow herself to relax into my touch, so I talk to get her mind to stop overthinking this. Because even with how little I know about Jenna Lewis, I know her mind is racing right now.

"Are you close with your brother, Trey?"

"As close as two siblings can be with our hectic careers and schedules." Her body eases as she talks. "When he lived in LA, things were easier, but I try to visit him in Tampa whenever possible, especially now that my parents moved out there too."

"He's getting married, right?"

"In two weeks, actually."

"I saw on the film schedule that we end just in time for you to travel to his wedding."

"Yes, I'm headed to Tampa. The wedding is on his yacht. It should be really nice." Her hand around my back shifts, moving up closer to my neck. "It's been a long time coming for him and Whitney. I'm really happy that everything worked out for them."

"And what about you? You said you want to get married. Does part of you wish it was you instead of him?"

"No, I'm happy for them. But I would like to get married sooner rather than later. It's in the five-year plan."

I smile. "You have a five-year plan?"

"Don't you?" She tilts her head toward me, brushing her cheek against the coarse hair on my beard.

"I have *a* plan, but there isn't a time limit by when it needs to be completed."

"Hmm." There's amusement in her voice. "I'd love to know what's in the mysterious Cody Banner life plan." Her fingers absentmindedly start stroking the back of my neck—a gesture that has my skin in flames. I close my eyes, focusing on and relishing in her simple touch.

"I'll tell you mine if you tell me yours."

Soft laughter puffs over her lips, leaving me wondering if, in the five months I've known her, I've ever elicited that feathery, sultry sound from her. "Okay, in five years, I want to be happily married with kids and have ten to fifteen movies under my belt. What about you?"

"What's in my life plan?" I open my eyes, sucking in a quick breath. "Right now, everything in my career is about image restoration, about appearing like a mature adult instead of the lovable playboy. That's why I hired Dallas Mikesell to be my manager and why I took the role in this Flixmart series." Her steps slow a little, as if she can't fully dance and listen to me at the same time. "This shift is important. It brings longevity to my career in the same way switching from modeling to acting helps you stay relevant longer. I'm hoping the tabloids, the media, the fans will talk about me for my acting and not for how late they think I stayed out or who I stayed out with."

Jenna slowly nods. "I didn't know you were trying to be someone different."

"I think I've been trying unsuccessfully since I was fourteen."

"I want people to see me differently, too. I want to be recognized for more than having a pretty face or a knock-out body. I want people to notice my talents or to compliment me on my intelligence."

"Sounds like we're both trying to break the stigma surrounding our names."

"I guess so."

"That's why I like acting. There are no stigmas or boxes. I get to become something different. Play the part of men who are better than me in real life."

"Tell me about it," Jenna breathes out the words.

My lips quirk. "You play men too?"

"No!" She swats the back of my neck, and I'm disappointed it breaks the tickling I'd grown to love. "I just like playing someone different than who I really am." Jenna's voice changes, and my breath stills a little, as if we both know the conversation is taking a vulnerable turn. "When I model, or even when I act, I get to be something more exciting. In real life, I'm boring and structured and not special at all. But when I step on a runway in a custom-made dress or pose for a picture, I become the sexiest woman alive. Every other woman wants to be me, and every man wishes he had me. It's a crazy-good feeling. The highest high. But when you remove all that glory and strip me down to just me, I'm a nobody."

My rocking stops, and I pull back to look Jenna squarely in the face. "What are you talking about? You're incredible."

She rolls her eyes and turns her head. "I'm not trying to

get compliments. I'm just saying people—*men*, really—think they're going home with Victoria's Secret but are disappointed when they learn I'm just Jenna."

"Hey." I touch my hand to her chin, forcing her to look at me. "Jenna is the version that has all the amazing qualities." She tries to shake her head, but I hold it firmly in place. "You're quick-witted and kind to people." I grimace. "Well, people who aren't me." She laughs, and I drop my hand, knowing I've kept it there too long. "And you're smart and talented."

My words are met with a pointed stare. "You're only saying that because I said I wanted to be recognized for my talent and intelligence."

"No, I'm being serious. You're smart, especially when it comes to film creation. You have a knack for spatial directions and camera angles. I actually think you'd make a great director someday."

Her stare softens. "You really think so?"

"I mean, I hate that I'm admitting it to you," I joke. "I was sure I would take these compliments to my grave. But yes, I really think you're talented and have a lot to offer Hollywood in front of the camera and behind it."

"No one, besides my brother, has ever given me credit for being more than something nice to look at, especially a man."

"Well, those men are idiots." I brush her hair back, not because I have to build chemistry but because I *want* to.

Jenna's green eyes flicker to my face like she's desperately trying to figure out my next move. To be honest, I don't know my next move. These are uncharted waters. Our position hasn't changed. My arm is around her waist, and hers is around my neck. Our hands are clasped together, resting against my chest.

But the emotions surrounding us have changed. There's a crackle in the air, popping between us. Our gazes are charged with developing attraction. I feel it in every heavy pulse of my heart.

My thumb draws slow circles over the skin at her waist, and despite our assumed lack of chemistry, our bodies pull together like we know just what to do. Eyes drop to lips, and before I can think through anything else, I dip my mouth to hers.

"Uh…" She completely pulls back, physically disconnecting herself from me. She pushes her lips into a sardonic smile, contradicting our honest conversation. "So this is how you do it?"

"What?" I'm genuinely confused right now.

Jenna takes a step back. "This is how you get women to fall for you?"

Oh.

Oh.

She throws in a mocking laugh with her smile, cutting my wound deeper. "You're really good at it. Like, *really* good. Props to your acting skills." Bending down to the lounge chair, she grabs her script. "If you do that during filming, Quinton will definitely be off our case on the whole chemistry thing."

"Right." I manage a smile. I am an actor after all.

"So, I think we're good here. Chemistry lesson complete. Yay!" She pumps her fists in the air as she walks toward the sliding doors. "Gold star for us." Pointing to where her room is, she says, "I'm just going to go shower. Answer some emails. Lay out on my balcony. So…"

Before I can say anything, Jenna escapes inside, leaving me standing alone by the pool.

We found our physical chemistry, but at what cost to my feelings?

CHAPTER
NINE

JENNA

CODY BANNER UNDERSTOOD THE ASSIGNMENT.

They said bring the heat. He brought it.

They said they wanted chemistry. He became a freaking STEM specialist.

They said they wanted our physical relationship to be so hot it would melt TV screens. So what did he do? He built the world's biggest inferno.

And I'm still reeling from it.

Eighteen hours and twenty-two minutes later.

That's right. I've managed to waste away the rest of our time in Malibu by ignoring, sunbathing, napping, and I even threw in watching *The Notebook*—for educational purposes. No one will ever be able to convince me that Ryan Gosling and Rachel McAdams hated each other when they started filming that movie. Their connection is too good to believe that.

And on top of everything I did, Cody was busy himself. His phone was on the kitchen counter, giving me the perfect glimpse of Calista James's face when she called him. He took the call outside on the deck, but it lasted forty-three minutes.

Forty-three minutes.

What on earth do two people have to talk about for forty-three minutes?

I'm not surprised, really. Of course Cody would almost kiss me and then be on the phone with his dirty mistress five hours later. I actually don't know if Calista is dirty or not. She seems like a lovely person from everything I've seen about her. But the adjective *dirty* just goes in front of *mistress*, thanks to Meredith Grey.

"Is that everything?" Cody asks as he lifts my suitcase from the back of his Jeep.

"Yep." I reach for the luggage.

"No, let me help you carry it to your door." He glances up at my two-story modern home nestled in Beverly Hills. "Nice place."

"Thanks." I beat Cody up the steps and punch in the code on my electronic keypad. The lock turns, and I spin around. "I can take it from here."

Our fingers slide over each other's as we make the pass off, and I'm reminded once again that touching him triggers every physical response in my body—normally a good thing unless you're trying to protect your heart from getting broken by the player who loves to play.

Cody doesn't retreat. Instead, his hands lazily go to his pockets, and his foot rests on the step above the one he's standing on. His chin lifts, and with his sunglasses on and that easy smile, he looks like something that just walked out of my deepest fantasy.

My love of the bad boy runs deep.

Too deep.

That's the thing about bad boys, or playboys, or whatever you want to call them. They have this whole vibe, from the swagger to the good looks to the never-ending confidence. It's my strongest weakness.

Pull it together, Jenna!

I cannot fall back into the same pattern of behavior. I need to get one of those shirts that say *Not today, Satan*. And in case you're wondering, Cody is Satan in this scenario—but a cute Satan, if that helps.

"I guess I'll see you tomorrow," I say, taking a step inside.

"Do you think our weekend in Malibu worked? Will Quinton be satisfied with the progress we made?"

I just dropped the biggest *get-lost* hint of all time, and it didn't even faze Cody. He's more interested in lingering chit-chat. I'd press charges for loitering if I actually thought that would get rid of him.

"Yeah, I think we'll be just fine."

"What flight to Calgary are you on?"

"Delta."

The drop in his expression makes me think he's disappointed. "Air Canada."

"Oh." I try to mimic his sad look.

At the sight of my next step inside, Cody gets the hint and backs down my front steps. "Okay, well. I guess I'll see you in Alberta."

"Sounds good." I give a little wave, then shut the door before he has the chance to come back.

I'M SPREAD out on my chaise lounge in my bedroom, watching Winnie pack my stuff for my flight. The early morning sunlight fills my entire room.

She pulls out a strapless hot-pink dress from my suitcase with raised eyebrows. "Did you wear this in Malibu?"

"And just where exactly did you expect me to wear that little number?"

"I don't know." Winnie shrugs, unable to stop her smile. "Out to dinner with Cody."

I give her a look that conveys all the reasons we just got

done discussing why I'm not sharing intimate dinners—or anything intimate—with Cody Banner.

"Alright, fine." She throws the dress aside. "I'll stop my wishful thinking that something will happen between the two of you."

"You need to. He's clearly with Calista James. I mean, you don't talk on the phone with a woman for forty-three minutes unless you really like them."

"Maybe they're just friends. Like Leo and Kate Winslet."

"Then why all the rumors that Cody broke up Calista's marriage?"

"They could just be rumors."

"Rumors are never just rumors. There's always a little bit of truth behind those stories."

Winnie rummages through my bag like she's searching for something. "What happened to those red wrap pants from Bali? I don't see them in here."

"They're gone."

"Gone? Where did—"

"Just gone." My palm lifts, stopping her right there. "And this time around, only pack tight pants, like leggings or something similar." I sit up, pointing at her for emphasis. "And don't pack anything sexy or revealing." I'm not taking any chances.

"Okay." She eyes me like I'm crazy, and I am.

Because in a couple of hours, I'll be in Alberta, on location, and when I get there, all my security measures go out the window.

It's my job to act like I'm in love with Cody.

CHAPTER
TEN

JENNA

ONE HUNDRED PAIRS of eyes zero in on me as I step out of the back of the car. It's like the entire cast and crew have been anxiously awaiting my arrival on set just to see if Cody and I have made progress.

There are even whispers and smirks. Whispers and smirks are never a good combination.

I discreetly glance down at my feet as I walk toward the trailers, checking to make sure I don't have toilet paper stuck to my shoe. Nothing's there.

"Hi, Jenna." Quinton's director's assistant, Naomi, greets me. "Everyone is waiting for you in Quinton's trailer."

"Okay." I smile at her while keeping a sharp eye on all the stares following me. "Why aren't they filming right now?"

Naomi turns over her shoulder, giving me a strange look. "Something came up, so we're taking a short break."

"What came up?"

"I'll let Quinton tell you."

The suspense is killing me. I have this foreboding feeling that I'm somehow to blame. Like maybe Cody told Quinton I avoided him the rest of the weekend after our little practice dance and almost kiss, and maybe Quinton got so mad he threw a camera or something, and now we can't film anything until new equipment shows up. It's all a stretch, but my mind won't stop running until someone tells me what's happening.

Naomi pulls open the door to Quinton's trailer and holds it for me. We share a glance as I pass by until my gaze focuses on the three people looking at me from inside the trailer. Quinton, Dallas, and Tawny have similar smiles covering their mouths that ease the foreboding feeling from moments ago.

But then there's Cody.

He's sitting on the couch, elbows on his knees, prayer hands by his chin, eyes down.

"Jenna!" Quinton cheers as I enter. "How was your flight?"

"Good." I let the door slam behind me.

"Take a seat." He gestures to the only available spot in the tight trailer, which happens to be next to Cody.

I catch Tawny's eyes, trying to glean what this little meeting is about, but all she does is smile at me as I sit down.

"What's going on?"

"She doesn't know," Quinton says to Tawny and Dallas.

Dallas shrugs. "Well, she's been on a flight. How could she?"

His words remind me my phone is still in airplane mode. But who even cares? At this point, it's easier to get information straight from the source.

My eyes bounce from one person to the next. "What don't I know?"

Tawny is the first to speak. "There's been a development."

"A development?" I glance at Cody again. I'm starting to get weirded out by his lack of response.

"A photographer captured pictures of you two in Malibu, and a story broke last night. It picked up traction and has gone viral."

It's the flipping pants!

Thanks to their good fortune, my bare butt has gone viral without any airbrushing, fancy cameras, or good angles. This is the worst.

That's why Cody looks so depressed.

He's embarrassed *for* me.

Tawny reaches inside her bag and pulls out a manila folder, opening it.

Great. We're going to look at the pictures right here and now. Fabulous.

She hands me the first one. I draw a steadying breath before dropping my eyes to the photo.

It's me.

And Cody.

On the balcony.

Arms wrapped around each other.

Lips millimeters apart.

The caption at the top reads: *Secret Lovers, Cody Banner and Jenna Lewis, Caught Getting Frisky in Malibu on a Break from Filming* The Promised Prince.

I stare at the words *Secret Lovers*, trying to rearrange them into something that actually makes sense. *Secret Enemies*, perhaps.

"The internet is going crazy with rumors that you and Cody are a couple."

An unedited picture of my butt would've been better than this. Surprisingly, that wasn't the worst thing after all. Being rumored to be in a relationship with Cody Banner is the worst thing.

I lift my eyes, staring blankly at Tawny. "But this isn't true." I frantically point at the picture. "We weren't even doing anything. Just practicing the upcoming scene." My gaze travels to Dallas and Quinton, finally landing on Cody. I nudge him with my knee. "Tell them we were just practicing."

He sits up. "Yeah, it was just practice."

"That was quite the practice," Tawny says in a voice that's a little too pleased if you ask me. She hands me picture after picture, all of Cody and me wrapped in each other's arms, looking cozier than the original Snuggie blanket.

"You have to tell them." I wave my hand at her and Dallas. "Release a statement saying that the rumors are false. We're not secret lovers."

"We're not doing that," Quinton says.

"Why?"

"Because it's good publicity for the show. And quite frankly, you two owe me."

"Quinton," Cody interjects, "I told you she wouldn't want to do it. Just let it go."

"Do what?"

Tawny placates me with her friendliest smile. "We all think it would be in the best interest of the show and the ratings if you two pretended to be a couple."

"No way!" I stand, pacing back and forth in the 2 x 2 area between the couch and the door. "You're talking about a fake relationship? A *show*mance between Cody and me?"

"A publicity stunt," Dallas corrects, as if his verbiage makes it all better.

"Some people in the business call it a love contract," Tawny offers.

"I know what it is. I just—"

"She just doesn't want to fake date me. Can you blame her?"

My gaze drifts to Cody and his low-hung head.

I sound like a brat. Like the rudest brat-jerk there ever was. He doesn't know my reasons for being adamantly against this plan. In his eyes, I hate him, so therefore, I hate the idea of being romantically linked to him.

The truth is, I'm scared.

My heart has been broken by a long line of men just like Cody Banner. Each time, I swore to myself that the *new guy* was different, that he wouldn't lead me on or leave as soon as the fun of dating a supermodel wore off. Each time, I was wrong.

I'm tired of being left behind by a man who never loved me.

I'm tired of making the same mistakes.

Albert Einstein wouldn't want me to do this. He said, "The definition of insanity is doing the same thing over and over again but expecting different results."

This plan is the definition of insanity.

I've learned the hard way. The playboy always breaks my heart. And pretending to be in love with one of them is like walking down a slippery slope. I can't *pretend* with Cody Banner. I'll lose my grip on reality and tumble down the showmance hill to the land of brokenhearted fools.

"Listen…" Quinton tries his hand at convincing me. "The first episode is getting a lot of bad reviews because of you two. The fake relationship takes the negativity away from the show and turns the buzz around to something exciting. We're already seeing the tide turn since the story broke. The positive ratings and viewing numbers of episode one have skyrocketed since last night. The pictures of you two in Malibu are everywhere, and everyone wants more." He looks directly at me. "Let's give them more."

"He's right." Tawny shrugs. "The celebrity gossip sites have been going nuts over you two. Your popularity and likability alone have gone through the roof overnight. Anyone who wasn't on board with your transition from modeling into acting is now your biggest champion of the change."

Dallas turns to Cody. "I don't even have to tell you the benefits this connection brings for you. Jenna is America's sweetheart, and in their minds, she has completely tamed the bad boy. It shows growth and maturity—something we haven't been able to achieve on our own."

Cody combs his fingers through his hair in exasperation.

"Yes, but you're all missing one major thing. Jenna doesn't want to do it."

"Do you want to do it?" I'm not sure I want to know the answer, but I can't take the words back now.

"I mean…" His broad shoulders lift and fall in the cutest boyish shrug I've ever seen.

"Fine," Quinton huffs. "If you two aren't willing to do this for your own careers, think about the cast and crew. We haven't been signed on for a second season with Flixmart yet. They're waiting to see if the show is a success. If you both do this, a second season is a given. Teague Morrow is counting on that. It means continual jobs for the cast and crew and yourselves. You'll be back for *The Stolen Princess* and *The Forgotten Queen.* Not to mention, my reputation as a director is on the line. But if all of that isn't enough, think about the author of the books the series is based on. You'd be fulfilling her lifelong dream by getting her books made into shows."

"Don't be a jerk, Quinton." Cody glares at him. "We all know what you're doing."

"What? I can't tell Jenna what's on the line if she doesn't agree to this?"

"You're manipulating her, and you know it."

Something about how Cody defends me scares me even more. Like, why can't he just stay the detached playboy jerk? It would make all of this so much easier.

"Jenna?" Tawny gets my attention through the noise. She gestures for me to sit down, and for some reason, I obey. "I know you pride yourself on being honest and genuine, and I respect that about you. But this would just be taking on another role. You'd be playing the part of a happy couple in order to promote the series. It's no different than playing Renna Degray in *The Promised Prince.*"

Except, this is real life with real feelings.

I drop my head into my hands, thinking over everything

they've said. If I don't do this, I run the risk of taking down the entire series, not to mention my career, Quinton's, and Cody's. I hate it, but I don't see any way out of this.

"You don't have to do this," Cody whispers next to me.

I lift my head, gazing into his vivid blue eyes. "Yes, I do." I swing stare around the room. "Fine. I'll do it. But I want an ironclad contract."

And if we could get something made of iron to lock my heart up, that would be helpful too.

"Oh, don't you worry, honey." Tawny pulls out a stack of papers from her purse and hands them to me. "I've already started working on the contract. But before we get into that, let's talk about tomorrow. I've scheduled an exclusive interview with *Celebrity Today* that will be broadcast on their evening show and their website."

"You already scheduled it?"

"That's correct." Tawny nods. "Their crew is on a plane headed to us as we speak."

"What if I had said no to this fake relationship? Then what?"

"I knew you wouldn't say no, because this is what's best for your career. We didn't work this hard for this many years just to give up now."

She's right. I may hate everything about this plan, but I can't say no to it even when I want to. There's too much on the line.

Quinton leans forward. "I think the exclusive is a great idea to keep people watching the series."

Tawny blinks back at him. "Of course it's a great idea. I came up with it. *Celebrity Today* will fly to Calgary. They'll do the entire interview here on location. It will be about *The Promised Prince*, but also your new relationship, so really make sure you sell that. Okay?" She looks back and forth between me and Cody, waiting for an answer.

She must get one from both of us, because she moves to the contract, but I don't remember saying anything. It's like I've just driven twenty blocks home and pulled into my driveway with absolutely no recognition of how I got there.

That's exactly what this whole experience is like.

I have no idea how I got here.

CHAPTER
ELEVEN

JENNA

THE CALL RINGS twice before my brother Trey picks up.

"I was wondering when I'd hear from you." His voice is full of amusement. He's obviously seen the tabloid stories.

Gossip really does travel fast.

"It's not true." After I say those words, I grimace, looking around to make sure my make-up artist didn't hear me. She's at the other end of the trailer, comparing different shades of lipstick to the dress I'm supposed to wear in the scene we're filming tonight.

Twenty minutes ago, in Quinton's trailer, I signed a contract with a non-disclosure clause stating that I can't tell anyone that Cody's and my relationship is fake. And here I am, already blabbing to my brother.

I suck at being fake.

And non-disclosure clauses.

"I don't know." Trey laughs. "Those pictures of you and Cody in Malibu looked pretty true to me. But I was kind of surprised by them. I thought Cody was dating Calista James. Didn't she leave her husband for him?"

Trey is alarmingly up to speed on celebrity gossip. But I didn't even think about the Calista James thing when I made this deal. In some ways, she makes this whole thing easier but also more awkward. I'm not sure how it accomplishes both of those things, but it does.

"It's a publicity stunt," I blurt so Trey knows I'm not crowding in on Calista's territory. "We're pretending to be a couple to help promote the series." I detach my voice from any feeling because if I let myself feel anything, I'll probably start crying.

"Wait. Like a fake relationship?"

My fingers slide over my brows as if that could somehow save me from my embarrassment. "Something like that."

Trey laughs. "When you said you were going to try your hand at acting, you really meant it. Mom and Dad are going to flip when they find out."

I sit up straight. "They're not going to find out, because you're not going to tell anyone that the relationship is fake. I'll be sued or fined or something really terrible if the information gets out."

"I'll keep my mouth shut."

"Forever!" I bark, sending all eyes in the makeup trailer to me. I smile and point to the phone. That's enough for everyone to go back to what they were doing.

"You have to pretend to be in a fake relationship with Cody Banner *forever*?"

"No." My entire body slumps farther into my chair. "Just until ratings for *The Promised Prince* go up and Flixmart has signed on the series for a second season."

"That sounds easy enough."

"Really? That's your response?"

"What do you want me to say?"

"I don't know. You're my older brother. Aren't you supposed to tell me how inappropriate and immoral this whole thing is, forcing me to stop it before it even begins?" I'm secretly hoping for that. Then I can go to Tawny and Dallas and tell them the entire fake relationship is off. My brother says it's unethical. Too bad. So sad.

"Jenna, you're an adult woman. You can make your own decisions yourself. But if someone is pressuring you into doing this, then…" His voice turns hard, "Wait, is Cody pressuring you to do this? Because if he is, I'm going to kill—"

"No!" I groan. "This arrangement is mutually beneficial for both of our careers, not to mention everybody involved in the series."

"So what's the problem, then?"

I bite my lip, glancing around again to make sure I'm out of earshot. "You know my dating history."

"Yeah."

"So you know I always fall for guys like Cody Banner."

"Douchebags who break your heart?"

"Exactly."

"That's in real life. This is fake, right? You'll be acting the whole time."

"What if all the fakeness turns to realness? I'll just get my heart broken all over again."

"Don't let that happen."

I wish he could see my eye roll. "That's easier said than done."

"I know, but what if you approach this like an acting job? Use it as practice. How would you play the part of a woman who isn't scared of falling for the playboy and getting her heart broken?"

"That woman would be confident and flirtatious, almost to the point of leading him on, not the other way around."

"Great. Assume that role whenever you have to be in the fake relationship."

Play the part of a confident woman? I've been doing that for years.

"Then, when you're out of the public eye, treat Cody like

you'd treat anyone else you're working with. It's an acting job. Turn it on for the cameras, then immediately turn it off when they stop rolling."

"What about Albert Einstein? He said—"

"I remember what he said because that's the only quote you ever quote. Thanks to you, we all know his definition of insanity by heart."

"The guy was a genius, Trey." I transfer my phone to the other ear. "It's unwise to ignore his advice."

"So don't expect a different result. Don't expect Cody to fall for you. Don't expect what he's saying and doing to be real. He'll be acting just like you. Everything about this situation is different than your past failed relationships because those were *relationships.* This is business to help boost your career. When you compartmentalize it like that, you take the real feelings away."

"You're right. This is business. We're both actors playing a role. Neither one of us wants or expects anything different. I'll be fine." Nodding accompanies each sentiment, an added layer to help convince my heart that Trey is right.

"And whatever you do, don't make rules."

"Why? Rules seem like they'd be a good idea to keep things professional."

"No, rules are made to be broken. The second you make them, it triggers your brain that those lines should be crossed and that you *want* to cross them. That's what happened with me and Whitney."

"Yeah, that makes sense, but there are general rules in our contract, like PDA in all forms is on the table whenever we feel it's necessary." That was a *very* important item in the contract for Quinton so that Cody and I could continue to build chemistry for these last few episodes. Plus, Tawny said the tabloids love juicy pictures of celebrity couples kissing in public and holding hands, so it was basically non-negotiable.

"And it's written in the contract that nothing intimate beyond PDA is allowed."

"Okay, that's a good rule. I know guys like Cody, and they only have one thing on their minds."

"He's not *really* like that—at least he doesn't want to be like that anymore."

"Look at you. You're already defending him after one day of being his fake girlfriend."

"I'm not defending him," I snap.

"Easy." Trey laughs. "I was joking."

"I know. Sorry." I shake my head, silently acknowledging that this whole fake-relationship has me on edge. "At least at the end of all of this, it will be a mutual, amicable breakup that both parties decided was for the best." I'm literally quoting the contract verbatim. "So, if nothing else, I won't walk away looking the fool like I have in the past."

"That's good. I don't want any of this to damage your reputation."

"Me too."

"When do you start? What's your first public outing? You're filming in Alberta now, right?"

My eyes drift around the trailer. "Yeah, I just flew in this afternoon. But Tawny wants to capitalize on the buzz from the Malibu pictures, so she set up an exclusive interview tomorrow morning with *Celebrity Today* so we can be interviewed together and confirm the relationship."

Butterflies drift through my stomach in the worst way.

"Does Tawny ever sleep?"

"I don't think so."

"Alright, an interview. So what? You've done hundreds of those before."

"Yeah, but never while pretending to be in love with my costar."

"That does throw a wrench in things, but I still think you've got this."

"How? I don't even know how to act during the interview or after that."

"Embody the confident, flirty woman who isn't scared of getting her heart broken. It's just another acting job."

"I'll try to remember that. What about you?" My mouth lifts. "How are the wedding plans coming?"

"Everything's coming together. We're getting down to it now. We're under two weeks."

"I'll be there."

"You better."

"Thanks for talking things through with me."

"Jenna, it's going to be okay. Don't let anyone push you around. Be the one that's calling the shots in this situation, and everything will turn out the way it's supposed to."

I love my brother's optimism.

I just wish I believed in his words as much as he does.

CHAPTER
TWELVE

CODY

THE NIGHT SKY at the base of the Canadian Rockies is
one of my favorite parts of being in a rural spot in Alberta.
Thousands of stars illuminate everything, and there's even the
added touch of crickets or some other kind of insect, giving
off that classic summery sound in the background.

I stand still in the middle of the garden as my stylist
finishes the final touches on my outfit for this scene. She tugs
on each sleeve, rolling them up past my elbows.

Naomi is behind the stylist's shoulder, going over some
last-minute directions from Quinton. "For this scene in the
garden, when Trev stumbles on Renna out here alone, it's
supposed to be somber—sad almost. The realization that
they're trapped in their lives and are losing each other really
weighs them down. Quinton wants you to deliver the lines in
Trev's charming way, but there needs to be a hint of sadness
behind every glance, touch, or word you say. A longing that
things could be different."

My eyes flip to her. "A longing that things could be
different?"

"Yes."

I nod, tuning Naomi out with my own thoughts.

Longing should be easy.

Ever since Jenna walked away from me on the balcony in Malibu, I've felt exactly that. I wished that we could start over, that my reputation hadn't preceded me or tainted her opinion of who I am before she even had the chance to get to know me.

It's too late for that.

She's pegged me as the player who only cares about getting women to fall for me. She's not wrong. I've been that guy. I *was* that guy. I just don't want to be him anymore.

But now, we're doing this whole fake-relationship thing, which normally wouldn't have been a problem for me. I would've gone along with whatever storyline Dallas conjured up and not thought twice about it.

But with Jenna, I am thinking twice.

She's not like the other women I've messed around with. There's a certain innocence to her reputation that I don't want to tarnish. It's like I've shown up muddy at an all-white house and touched everything with my dirty hands.

I glance to where Jenna sits in a director's chair, getting her makeup touched up. She's wearing a cream vintage dress that's a cross between medieval and bohemian with metallic embellishments that trim the neckline and sleeves. She looks beautiful in it, as she should. I mean, she's not a supermodel for nothing. But it's more than her flawless face and perfect body.

There's a warmth behind her smile that's genuine, making you feel like she could be your best friend. I rarely get to see it used on me, but when I watch her with others, it's what draws people in. I admire her openness in how she greets cast members and strangers with clasped hands and kisses on their cheeks. Personally, I'd never do that, but I like that everyone she meets starts on the same level as her.

Except for me.

I never started on Jenna's level—and rightfully so. She's the perfect sweetheart, and I'm the guy who's made every single mistake in the book. Those two things don't go together. We're the human equivalent of water and oil.

But even knowing this, I can't shake that I *felt* something the other day on the balcony when I held her. This intense desire to be better. To become better *for* her. To behave in a way that *earns* her respect.

Son of a—!

I shake my head. Where did all of these stupid, sissy thoughts come from? Wait. I know. This whole thing is Dallas's fault with his ridiculous image-restoration plan. My head is so mixed up with 'be a better man' lingo that now I'm projecting it onto my working relationship with Jenna.

I just need everyone to think I'm a better person so I can continue working in this industry and stay relevant in the public's eye.

Right? That's what I'm doing all this for.

Yeah, that sounds right.

"I think those are all the notes Quinton wanted me to tell you." Naomi flips through her script, jarring me out of my pathetic thoughts.

"Sounds good, thanks." I hope I didn't miss anything important when I wasn't listening.

Quinton walks on set, turning to look at the entire crew as he speaks. "Are we ready to work?"

Jenna hops out of her chair, walking to where I stand.

"I like your costume," I say, breaking the ice. Lately, every interaction I've had with her is me trying to break the ice. I'm basically carrying around a pickaxe like how other men carry pocket knives.

Her eyes sweep over her dress. "I think the pretty clothes are the best part of working on this show."

"I thought for sure you were going to say working with me was the best part."

Why am I flirting with her? She's not interested. *I'm* not interested. I'll just chalk it up to building chemistry. Everything can go under that umbrella.

"You wish working with you was the best part," she mutters with a small smile.

I'll take that as a win.

"Let's see how well my little experiment worked this weekend." Quinton walks toward us, draping his arms over both of our shoulders, leading us farther into the garden. "I have a really good feeling about this next scene. And if your chemistry is anything like those pictures from Malibu, then we're in for a treat."

Jenna's gaze flicks to me and then down to the ground.

Quinton releases us and spins around, looking at the crew of over one hundred and fifty people. "Renna is sitting on the cement wall in the garden, talking to her father but really to herself because he's dead. We just filmed that scene." He nods at Jenna as if she wasn't already aware of what they just filmed. "Trev's going to walk in"—he gestures to the pathway that leads into the garden—"say his lines, and join her sitting on the wall." Quinton shifts his gaze to me. "Naomi went over the notes with you on the overall vibe of the scene?"

"Yeah, I think I've got it." Mostly. I got a little sidetracked thinking about Jenna.

"Good. Everything should be cut and dry with blocking since the two of you aren't really moving, and there's no touching."

No touching.

Something about that is very disappointing.

There's the longing again.

I *long* to touch Jenna, and since I can't touch her in real life or in our chemistry practice lessons, all I'm left with is the show, which is unfortunate since my character is engaged to be married to another character who isn't Jenna's. Rough life.

Quinton turns and looks at the cameramen. "I want to go

through a few last-minute changes with camera angles and lighting." He shouts some commands, ignoring Jenna and me completely.

"Hey"—I lean in so we can have a private conversation, dismissing how the closeness sends my body into overdrive— "I'm sorry about the pictures and the story about us being in a secret relationship. If I had known there were paparazzi in Malibu, I never would've touched you like that."

Or touched you like that and *liked* it.

"You make it sound like we were caught in bed together." She smirks, spinning my stomach into a tornado. "Last I checked, we were just dancing."

And we almost kissed, but clearly, Jenna wants to block that part out of her mind. Honestly, so do I—selective memory at its finest—because at that moment, things felt really real to me.

"Right, it was just a dance." I shrug it off.

"Besides, I was the one that suggested we go outside, so there's nothing for you to apologize about."

"And now we're dating, *not* in secret." I scratch my forehead. "That's going to be crazy, huh?"

Huh? My insecurity and need for her approval is pathetic.

"We're actually *fake* dating," she corrects. "And as far as I'm concerned, it will just be an extension of *The Promised Prince.* We'll play the part of two people who enjoy each other's company in a romantic way. Jenna, Renna—it's all the same, and it rhymes."

"Don't let the trio hear you say that, or they'll send us back to Malibu to work on our chemistry again."

"True." Jenna's laugh comes out through her nose with a snort, but it's cute. I find pretty much everything she does to be really cute.

"Well, thanks for agreeing to the love contract thing or whatever you want to call it. I think it'll help generate positive press for the series."

It's weird thanking a woman for basically just tolerating me, but maybe that's part of transitioning from a boy to a man—you realize that women mostly just tolerate you, and you're grateful for whatever crumb they throw your way.

"It's not a big deal." Jenna smiles, and the warmth I mentioned earlier is acutely absent from her eyes as she stares back at me. "It's just acting. Like any other day on set. And when we're not acting, we'll go our separate ways like we normally do."

I'm noticing a pattern. It's obvious Jenna wants me to know she considers the fake relationship as part of the job. Nothing more. There's a precedence being set, and I hear the message loud and clear.

"Definitely," I puff out. "I feel the same way," I huff. When does huffing and puffing become too much? Because I think I've entered that territory. I'm about to become a member of the Three Little Pigs.

Jenna runs her fingers through her hair impassively, and I mentally tell myself it's not the cutest thing I've ever seen. "Also, be sure you tell Calista that it's all just for show."

My lips drop into a frown. "As in *Calista James*?"

Her green eyes drift to me. She's trying to keep them impassive, but I think I see a flash of jealousy, or more precisely, I *hope* I see a flash of jealousy. "Yeah, you were talking with her on the phone the other day, right? You're together."

I don't know if that was a question or a statement, but I clarify just in case it's a question. "We're just friends."

"Either way." More impassiveness. "I just don't want her to think I'm romantically interested in you in real life."

I have to hand it to Jenna. She can innocently throw a knock-out punch without breaking a sweat. I actually like that about her.

"Calista is a non-issue." I tilt my head toward her, effort-lessly inching my body even closer. I get a whiff of strawberry, and my eyes snap to the pink on her lips. Strawberry lip gloss. I bet that would taste amazing against my tongue.

Nope, Cody. Save those thoughts for when we're filming. Or for never. Never have those thoughts.

I reluctantly pull my gaze back to her eyes. "But feel free to tell your boyfriend I'm not romantically interested in you in real life either."

And if I could know exactly who he is, that would be really helpful for when I hunt him down and kill him.

Jenna lifts her chin, shaking her hair back from her face. "That's a non-issue as well."

Meaning she *doesn't* have a boyfriend? That makes my life easier. Manslaughter is messy and highly inconvenient.

But now, I am suddenly very curious about Jenna's dating history. I can't recall hearing her name paired with anyone in my circle. I only know what she told me in Malibu—men think they're going home with Victoria's Secret and are disappointed when they realize it's just her.

Who cares about the fantasy on the billboard? The real-life woman standing in front of me is pretty incredible.

"Cody, that's when the camera will swing to you as you say your last line."

I tear my eyes away from Jenna and focus on Quinton's instructions.

"I'd love a sad smile here or something that lets the viewer know how heartbroken you are that you can't be with this woman. Then we'll zoom in on Renna as she watches Trev walk away." He looks between the two of us. "Does that sound good?"

"Yep," we say in unison.

"Great." Quinton heads for his director's chair. "Let's get started."

I walk to the edge of the garden path, where I begin the scene. A team works around Jenna, fanning her dress around her as she sits on the cement wall.

A pulse of excitement hangs on every beat of my heart. It's been a long time since I've felt something like this while filming. The last few years, I've just gone through the motions of acting, but today, the love of the job has somehow found its way back into my veins, and for the first time since I started this show, I'm actually excited to film a scene.

The crew clears out as everything silences.

"Roll camera." Quinton nods at the camera operator to hit the record button.

"Rolling," he says back.

Quinton's finger circles through the air. "Roll sound."

"Rolling," the audio director replies.

The camera assistant steps in front of the camera with a slate. The sticks are held wide, making it look like an open-mouthed Pac-Man. She yells out, "Scene 21E. Take one." Then she closes the sticks of the slate, making a loud noise before moving out of the line of the camera.

Quinton calls, "Action!"

That's my cue.

I easily slip into my role as Trev, the prince of Albion, and casually walk toward Jenna—er, *Renna Degray*. I let my gaze stay on her, and my expression lightens in reaction to how peaceful she looks. Was that my acting or a natural response to her beauty?

"Well, aren't you a nice surprise," I say, infusing my voice with...actually, who am I kidding? I didn't have to infuse my voice with anything. Jenna has become a nice surprise.

Her eyelids lift, and even from across the garden and with the camera boom hanging above, I feel the weight of her stare tunnel through me like an electric wave. She's acting, of course. But underneath what she's bringing to the role of Renna is a dose of herself.

"How did you find me?"

"I wasn't looking for you." I let my smile fill with amusement as I continue toward her. The camera slowly moves backward with each of my steps.

"Of course not. I was just—"

"Don't get me wrong. I'm happy to stumble upon you," I cut her off as I approach the cement wall. "I was really taking a walk. I do that sometimes when I need to think." The camera above swings with me as I turn my body and hoist myself up onto the ledge. In my eagerness to touch her, I get a little too close and end up sitting on the edge of her thigh.

She breaks character and laughs. "Are you trying to sit in my lap?"

I hop down, turning to Jenna with a sultry smile. "Are you requesting a lap dance?"

"Oh, my gosh!" She kicks her leg out to me in a flirty way. "We're in the middle of a scene." Her response is different from how it was while filming the first three episodes. Back then, an innuendo comment from me like that would've evoked a major eye roll and a glare from her, but post-Malibu, Jenna playfully kicked me. We're making progress.

"Alright." I roll my finger over and over to Quinton and the cameraman. "Let's try that again."

"I was just taking a walk," Naomi calls, reminding me what line to start with.

I nod, flipping into my role once again. "I was really taking a walk. I do that sometimes when I need to think." This time, when I lift my body up on the ledge, I nail the perfect position with my thigh pressed against Jenna's. "What about you? What brings you out here?"

"I was just missing my dad and wanted to talk to him." She turns to me with the most adorable, sheepish smile I've ever seen. "He's a great listener."

"I bet he is." I relax in my spot, getting comfortable with the scene. "What was he like?"

Jenna flawlessly dives into a monologue about her pretend dad. I should probably be listening so I know when to deliver my next line, but instead, I notice every little detail and nuance about how she talks and how her gaze drifts to a spot just beyond me. I wonder if that's how she's playing Renna or if the faraway look is because she's trying to remember her lines as she says them. I'm regretting now that I wasted the last five months being standoffish when I could've been memorizing every last detail about her.

Jenna's gaze drifts to me, and for a moment, I get lost in her green eyes—that is, until her gaze turns expectant.

"He sounds pretty amazing," Naomi shouts, hoping to jar my memory.

"Right, thank you." Both Jenna and I reset. "He sounds pretty amazing."

"He was. You're a lot like him."

She smiles, and dang, she has a good smile, but I've already been distracted enough, so I force myself to stay present in the scene and deliver my next line.

"Me?" I feign modesty. "Probably not, but I'll take the compliment. How did he die?"

She goes through her next part, and again, I'm trying to stay focused, but it's so hard when she looks so devastatingly sweet. Did she always look this good while filming, or did some magical elf sneak into her trailer before filming tonight and sprinkle dust on her to make her absolutely irresistible to me?

Had to be an elf—only plausible answer.

We go back and forth with our parts. Aside from a few slip-ups on our lines and some bad camera positions, everything goes smoothly. Usually, by now, Quinton has yelled, "CUT!" five or six times, and we've needed five or six breaks to get through a scene together, but tonight, we've managed to keep going with minimal stops.

I'm coming up on the end of my character's sad childhood-trauma monologue. I think it went pretty well. A messed-up childhood is something I can easily relate to. I say my last line about how I haven't felt loved since Queen Avina died and am shaken to the core when Jenna places her hand over mine. Quinton said there wasn't any touching in this scene, but he forgot about the handhold. So did I until her touch sent warm shivers up my arm.

I stare back at Jenna, wondering if she feels what I feel, the inexplicable sensation that something more than on-screen chemistry is happening here. A flash of attraction rages through her eyes, building tangible heat between us.

"I've been thinking about what you said," Naomi prompts, as if the pause is just from me forgetting my next line.

Jenna drops her eyes, breaking our shared fascination. But I don't want to lose what's building, so I nudge her chin with the tip of my finger, prodding her gaze to mine before I dive back into the scene. Her green eyes light with the same passion from before. Unspoken chemistry.

We exchange lines back and forth until I get to one specific line. I remember the notes from the table read. I'm supposed to be vulnerable when I deliver this part. There's something achingly personal about this moment that feels real, that brings raw vulnerability.

"Sometimes I think about how things between us might've been different if I wasn't"—*a playboy*—"the prince." My eyes search Jenna's, hoping for some indication that she's ever thought this about us too.

Her brows raise. "Or marrying Seran?"

My hopes drop. Jenna is not reading between the lines for some shared real-life connection to the story and characters we're playing.

She's acting.

We're both just acting.

I mask my expression and drop my eyes. "Yes, or marrying Seran."

"Aren't there any loopholes in this arranged-marriage thing?" Jenna puffs out a self-conscious laugh. "I mean, if you're elected to royalty, and it's not a bloodline thing, why does marrying a princess even matter?"

My eyes glance away. "It's more about *who* Seran is. Not what. She's—"

"Keep rolling!" Quinton yells, then looks directly at me. "Cody, can we get more here? You guys have had mind-blowing chemistry this entire scene up until now. I don't know what happened, but you look completely detached all of a sudden."

I'll tell you what happened. I realized this was all fake.

Jenna was acting the entire time.

And she was *good* at it. No, great, actually. She had me believing there was actually a connection between us.

"Sorry." I let go of her hand and rub my eyes.

"You're fine," Quinton says. "Just get back into the groove of chemistry again. Let's take it from, 'She's the daughter of the king,' blah blah blah." Quinton leans forward, looking down at his notes. "And Cody, switch your hands here so you're holding on top. That way, you can draw circles on her skin with your thumb."

Yeah, why not just pour salt into my wound?

"You bet," I mutter.

I grab Jenna's hand, catching her eyes as I do. Our fingers fumble together like I'm declaring a thumb war.

Real smooth.

"My hand is supposed to be on top," Jenna explains, "since that's how the scene ended, and then you can transition to the other way once you say your lines."

Great, now I look like the newbie here.

"Let's start again," Quinton says, and the crew quiets.

"She's the daughter of the king of New Hope." My voice cracks as I say the line like some fourteen-year-old boy going through puberty. I shake my head and clear my throat, avoiding Jenna's gaze.

I'm sure she's loving this.

I take a deep breath and flip back into character, saying my line again so post-production has a clean place to start. I glance up at her, not missing the amusement behind her eyes —yep, she's loving it. But her playfulness puts me at ease and helps me finish what I'm supposed to say. Seamlessly, I change the position of our hands, allowing me to slowly trace her knuckles with my thumb. Warmth spreads throughout my body as if I'm eighty years old and sleeping under a freaking electric blanket.

I've got problems.

And I'm not even at the best lines of the scene yet, but I'm already dreading them. No, I'm dreading my *reaction* to them. But I'm a professional, so I throw caution to the wind and dive headfirst into the last little bit, and when it's time for me to give it my all, my body leans toward hers like she's pulling me in with a reel. I smell that same strawberry lip gloss and say what I'm supposed to say.

"I would tell you every day how beautiful you were and how much I loved being with you." Jenna swallows, and I hate not knowing if that's her response to me or Renna's response to Trev. When did acting become so complicated? But I keep going. "I would never take you for granted." I say those words, fully knowing that I've been a complete fool the last five months, taking her for granted every single day.

After what I would consider a few seconds of heated glances back and forth, Jenna removes her hand from mine and tucks her knees up to her chest. She eyes me with a sad smile. "We would have been pretty amazing."

"I think so." I'm surprised by how real my own sadness feels. "I guess we'll never really know." And that's how it is in real life too. I'll never really know if Jenna Lewis and I could've been something more than costars who barely got along. I ruined my chances with her long ago and every day since.

My lips press downward as that realization washes over me.

Hold up.

I'm supposed to be Trev right now.

Full of sadness, regret, and longing.

But I'm already those things.

I glance at the ground in embarrassment until I remember everyone here thinks I'm acting, not sad in real life because I'm starting to wish that things between Jenna and me could be different. That *I* could be different.

"I guess I'll let you get back to your conversation with your dad." I scoot off the edge, sending her one last sad smile before starting my walk out of the garden. "Tell him I said hi."

"Cut!" Quinton yells, and just like that, the moment is over.

CHAPTER
THIRTEEN

JENNA

TAWNY POPS her head in my trailer. "Two minutes until the interview."

"Okay, thanks."

"I'll meet you over there." She lets the door shut behind her.

I slowly rise to my feet, placing my hands on my hips as my head hangs low. Nerves spin inside my stomach. The kind I used to get before every fashion show or runway event. The kind that make me feel like I'm not good enough to be doing what I'm doing. Whether it's walking a catwalk in front of thousands or being a good enough actor to pull off this fake-dating charade.

I hate that my inadequacy is always the last thing that floats through my mind. When everything else is silent, my insecurities are loud and upfront.

I lift my head and draw in a deep breath, resigned to not only fake my relationship today but to fake my confidence.

Because that's what it takes to make it in this industry.

I place my phone on the bed and walk out of the trailer at, coincidentally, the same time Cody exits his.

He looks extra handsome this morning in a fitted collared shirt that's snug over his shoulders and biceps.

His lips slowly peel into a smile, barrel-rolling my stomach. "Are you ready for this?"

"Yep." My voice is cheery and bright, channeling my fake confidence. I'm cool, calm, and collected—the three Cs. "Are you ready for it?"

Cody's steps fall in stride with mine as we walk toward where the interview has been set up. "Am I ready to show people how madly in love with you I am?" His lips curve up on one side. "I've never been more ready for anything in my life."

Great.

He's flirty today.

I'm filing that information in the back of my mind to remind myself in case things start to go bad during the interview—and by *things*, I mean rogue feelings coming to the surface.

There's an undeniable push and pull between us that I wish didn't exist. My heart is constantly living in a tug-of-war game between enemies and something more, wondering which one will win out.

Filming last night was *hard*. It's the touching that gets me.

Every. Single. Time.

Cody's body is a conductor, transferring electric charges into me with the slightest finger brush or hand hold. When the garden scene was over, I was like one of those mad scientists with my hair sticking straight up and smoke drifting away from my head.

I barely made it out alive.

How am I supposed to survive a filmed interview as his fake girlfriend? Talk about a baptism by fire on your first day on the job.

"Listen, I understand if it's too hard for you to fake feelings for me. I can take the lead on this one."

I pause, thinking over his words for a second. They weren't meant to be patronizing, but when combined with my nerves and my lack of confidence, they rub me the wrong way.

I double-step to catch up to him. "You don't think I can do it?"

"No, that's not what I meant. I'm just saying I know that I'm not your favorite person, so conjuring up feelings of love might be difficult. If you want to take a backseat on this one, I'll drive."

There isn't any smugness behind his eyes or in his expression, but I'm still bugged.

"I don't need to conjure up feelings for you. I'm an actor, and this is part of my job. I'm prepared to deliver the most lovey-dovey couple the media has ever seen."

I'm taking Trey's advice and *acting*, playing the part of a bold, confident woman.

Cody's dark brows cinch together, contradicting the slight smile on his lips. "The most lovey-dovey couple the media has ever seen? Is that what you want people to think about us?"

"Why not?" I lift my chin, my confidence on a roll. "If we're doing this, we might as well do it right."

"Okay, if that's what you want." There's humor behind his voice, but I don't glance over at him, just keep walking full steam ahead. I'm surprised he can even keep up.

"So, should we talk strategy real quick?"

"Strategy?" The cameras and lighting are ahead, with a crew from *Celebrity Today* checking everything. A couch and a single chair are set up for the interview. In the background, the giant manor we've been filming at stands tall with a clear blue sky and green fields surrounding it. I keep walking, just wanting to get this interview over with as fast as I can.

"Yeah, a strategy. Like, what's our dating story?"

Our dating story is that I'm completely attracted to you for all the wrong reasons, but you absolutely can't know that, and I am absolutely not falling for you, even if it means I make myself crazy denying it.

It's very complex.

I turn to him with a tight smile. "Let's just keep things simple."

"Okay, what's simple?"

Oh, now he wants to play twenty questions.

"You know, stay as close to the facts as we can. We met on set, and things progressed while filming."

"And what level of touching and flirting are we doing during the interview?"

My feet trip up, one over the other.

Cody grabs my shoulders before I faceplant, and as soon as I'm stable enough to stand on my own, I wiggle out of his arms. It's the *mention* of his touch that put me here in the first place. I pass off my stumble by immediately turning over my shoulder and looking at the ground where I just stepped.

"There's a hole there," I say loudly, pointing to the flat grass. "Someone's going to break an ankle." I glance at a few crew members standing around. "Let's get that taken care of before someone hurts themselves." They look at me like I'm crazy, but one guy takes a step forward, pretending to search for it—a valiant effort.

"You okay?" Cody asks.

"Yep, just fell in a hole." I brush my hair back from my face even though it's in a ponytail slicked so tight the force of Niagara Falls couldn't undo it.

"So, the touching and flirting?"

He's relentless on this subject, but this time, I'm able to stay upright.

My face goes void of emotion. I'm a robot repeating Trey's advice. "There are no rules. We're just acting. It's all for show."

His smile is loaded with amusement. "No rules?"

"That's right." I nod as we approach the interview spot.

"If that's what you want." He leans in, tickling my ear with his whispers. "You asked for it."

136

My spine straightens, and my gaze whips to him. "Asked for what?"

But before he can answer, Marley Lopez from *Celebrity Today* stands in front of us with a proffered hand. "Welcome! It's so nice to see you both."

Outwardly, I'm giving air kisses to each of Marley's cheeks. Inwardly, I'm screaming at Cody.

ASKED FOR WHAT?

CODY

I STAND in front of the couch as a makeup assistant dabs powder over my face.

"That should help with the heat and sweat," she says in between her chews of green gum.

"You know what else would've helped with the heat and sweat?" I ask rhetorically. "Filming this interview inside."

She laughs, opening her mouth so wide I'm worried her gum will fall out onto my shirt.

I lift my brows in response, then turn my attention to Jenna. She's next to me, getting a microphone wired through her shirt. Her hair is pulled back into a high ponytail that perfectly works with her halter neckline, hot-pink blouse. I say it perfectly works because the updo shows off her shoulders and the edge of her collarbone in the most flattering way.

"I think we're ready to begin." Marley takes the seat across from us.

The crew and assistants clear out, and Jenna and I drop onto the couch. I purposely sit right next to her, wrapping my arm around her shoulders and snuggling her in close.

She looks at me with raised brows. "It's, like, a hundred degrees outside. Do you think I can get a little space here?"

"I like keeping you close." I add a small wink, just for the fun of it.

"Look at you two!" Marley gushes. "You look so cozy."

"Too cozy." Jenna fake laughs while concealing the small pinches she's giving my side. I grab her crab fingers with my free hand, holding them on top of my leg so she can't do any more pinching damage.

Marley watches us with a giant smile. "So the rumors are true? You're an official couple?"

"Yes. We. Are." I lift our joined hands, bopping Jenna's nose with the tip of her own index finger as I say each word in my best baby voice.

I'm overdoing it.

I know I am, but Jenna asked for this with all of her *there are no rules* garbage.

There has to be rules, especially with the touching. Because if left up to me, I'd be all over the woman. They'd have to pry her out of my arms with a pair of pliers, and I'm guessing she wouldn't like that—the touching, not the pliers.

So, I'm using this interview to prove a point.

I'm all over her like white on rice.

When I'm through with her, she'll be begging me to put rules in place.

"How long have the two of you been together?" Marley asks.

We answer at the same time, me saying a couple of weeks and Jenna saying a couple of months. Our heads flip to each other, and her wide-eyed gaze tells me she's probably wishing she'd gone over strategy a little bit more.

Jenna backpedals with an overdone laugh. "I mean, the tension between us has been building for months, but we didn't act on it until a couple of weeks ago."

I squeeze her shoulder as I tug her in closer. "That's right."

She doesn't even look at me, just keeps her eyes trained on Marley.

"And what happened a couple of weeks ago that turned the tide?"

Jenna opens her mouth to answer, but my shushing finger covers her lips. "I'll take this one." I send an air kiss in her direction before turning to Marley.

Stay close to the facts. That's what she wants.

"I was attracted to Jenna from the moment I met her. She's classy, smart, beautiful, feisty, and kind. Who wouldn't fall head over heels for her?" Her head slowly turns to me as I talk, but I keep my focus on Marley. "But my reputation preceded me. She wasn't interested, and to top it off, she didn't even like me."

"So what did you do?"

"I did what every mature man would do. I acted like I didn't like her either."

Marley chuckles at that, but Jenna holds still, watching, listening.

"But the more I got to see the real Jenna, with nothing obscuring my view, the more tangled up in her I became. Like shoelaces in a bike wheel."

Marley smiles. "I love that metaphor."

"Me too. It really shows a lot." I start stroking the side of Jenna's arm with the hand wrapped around her shoulder. "We're just two people stripped naked of all the pretenses that were covering us up."

"So romantic," Marley gushes.

"Isn't it?" Jenna's smile is tight.

"And did the same happen for you once you got to know Cody better?" Marley's eyes flip to her.

"You know, Cody puts on this tough-guy persona in front of the cameras, but really he's such a sweetheart. He'd give you the shirt off his back."

"Hmm. That does sound like me." I nod, liking how Jenna

picked up on the inside joke. I don't know how she could've missed it. I literally put it on a platter for her.

She turns to me with a goofy smile. "Yes, it does."

I take the opportunity to thread my fingers through hers. She fidgets with her other hand like our position makes her a little uncomfortable, but this interview gives me a free hall pass to touch her, and I'm not wasting it.

"So you've been dating in secret for a few weeks?"

"Best few weeks of my life." I nuzzle my nose into her neck for added effect. When I lean back to my spot, my eyes catch Tawny behind the cameras, giving me a double thumbs up. She's clearly enjoying the show.

"That's correct, Marley." Jenna smiles, laying it on thick. "How can I resist a man like Cody Banner? He's not rumored to be good with the ladies for nothing, if you know what I mean."

I shoot her a stare, conveying that one was a low dig, but she just smiles sweetly back at me. It's time to get even with her.

"But I don't want it to be a secret anymore. I want the whole world to know this. Woman. Is. Mine." I ram her shoulder into me with each word. She's a pinball, bouncing back and forth between my hand and the crook of my arm. "Because when you find someone as genuine as her, you don't let her go." I squeeze her arm even tighter.

"Well, I certainly think all the world knows. Since those pictures of you two went viral Sunday night, you're the number one trending thing on the internet. We're all dying to get a glimpse of our favorite couple."

"Here we are." Jenna tries shrugging, but I'm holding her so close her shoulders can't really move up and down.

"Here." I kiss her cheek. "We." I kiss it again. "Are." I kiss it one last time.

I'm so obnoxious, and I don't even care.

Jenna eyes me with an are-you-kidding-me look, but I

don't regret anything. I'm having more fun in an interview than I ever have.

"Let's talk about *The Promised Prince.*" Marley holds her hands up. "We're in Alberta on location for the filming of the rest of the series. It's breathtaking here."

"It really is." Jenna relaxes into my arm as she talks, and suddenly, the charade doesn't feel so fake anymore—especially with the very real humming in my heart.

JENNA

THE *CELEBRITY TODAY* interview is a lot like blow-drying hair.

Specifically, like when you flip your head over and build a cave of wet hair around your face. You put the blow dryer in the center, angling the hot air at your scalp, thinking you're doing a great job getting your roots dry. Then suddenly, everything goes wrong, starting with a concerning whirling noise. A few strands of hair get sucked into the fan at the *back*, and now your hair is being ripped from your scalp by 1,875 watts of a Conair blow dryer. The only way to make it stop is by turning the machine off and yanking your hair out of the fan.

Well, I can't turn this interview off—or, for that matter, my raging heart.

That's why when Marley smiles and says, 'Those are all my questions,' and I give all the necessary thanks, I bolt out of there faster than the kid from *The Incredibles.*

"Jenna, wait." Cody is hot on my trail, which is terrible because he's the one making me *hot.* I have long legs, but even my strides can't hold him off. Within seconds, he's right next to me, his shoulder and arm against mine as we walk together.

He grabs my hand, and I turn to him, yanking it away.

"What are you doing?"

Cody's smile glows. "Everyone is still watching us, bumpkins. It would be nice if they didn't see us fighting."

Fine. I let him hold my hand as I keep walking.

"*Bumpkins?* Do I look like the type of woman who should be nicknamed *bumpkins?*"

"Would you prefer poopsie?"

I shake my head, still stuck on the first horrific term of endearment. "I don't even think bumpkins is a real word."

"It's probably not." He swings our joined hands between us, and it's so natural that it's annoying.

"And what was all that back there?"

"An interview?" His voice goes high, like he's unsure if he answered my question with the right answer. He didn't.

"I'm talking about *all* the touching. You mauled me during the entire thing."

"I was just being an affectionate boyfriend."

Affection is the last thing I need between us.

"Well, it was too much."

"Nah." He presses his lips into a disbelieving frown as he shakes his head. "You said you were prepared to deliver the most lovey-dovey couple the media has ever seen. I was meeting you halfway."

"Did you just quote me verbatim?"

"I have an excellent short-term memory, and I also remember you saying this fake relationship has no rules."

My chin lifts. "It doesn't."

Smugness overtakes Cody's expression. "Then why are you so upset about how the interview went?"

"I'm not upset. I'm just not the type of woman who enjoys PDA and being called bumpkins."

"In fairness, I didn't call you bumpkins during the interview, but I kind of wish I had. I think it really could've gained us some traction. It could've stuck."

I bite back my smile and don my poker face. "And by the way, you betrayed me back there."

"How?"

"By broadcasting my most embarrassing moment to Marley and every single viewer that watches *Celebrity Today*."

"Poopsie, I was just leaning into our inside joke. It's cute that we have one."

"No." I push my shoulder into him. "You can't use poopsie either."

"I'm just testing it out. You said there are no rules."

I know what I said.

"You're right." I relax my body—just more acting. "We need to convince everyone that we're crazy about each other."

Cody's brows and lips lift simultaneously. "So there's no problem?"

Why does he look so amused?

"Nope."

"There are my two lovebirds." Tawny leans between us, placing her hands on our backs, forcing us to walk and talk. I use her interruption as a way to drop Cody's hand without seeming like I'm not complying with the fake-relationship terms. "Cody, you stole the show in the interview."

"What about me? I did good too."

"Yeah, but Cody really shined."

"Thanks, Tawny. I rehearsed a lot of that in the mirror this morning."

Tawny's finger whips out, pointing to him. "That's what I'm talking about. Dedication to your role." She looks at me. "You should try that."

I can barely contain my eye roll.

"The key now is to keep the momentum going. Dallas and I have set up a brunch for you tomorrow."

"Tomorrow? What about filming?" And what about my freaking heart? I don't think I can take much more of this.

"Don't worry." Tawny flips my concerns away with the brush of her hand. "I've already talked to Quinton. He thinks brunch is a fabulous idea, leading us into the release of episode two. If all goes as planned, the pictures from your outing will be online the day before episode two airs." She drops her arms from our backs but keeps walking. "My photographers will be there getting pictures of you being chummy, and then I'll release them to a few reputable news sources, making sure they get splashed all over the internet and magazines. It'll be perfect."

"I'm game, and Jenna was just telling me how much she enjoyed that and wants to do it again." Cody leans over Tawny, eyeing me with a goofy smile. "Isn't that right?"

"That's actually not what I said. I—"

"You said, *verbatim*,"—he shoots me an arrogant glance—"'We need to convince everyone that we're crazy about each other.'" That arrogant gaze shifts to Tawny. "So the way I see it, we'd love to have brunch together."

"Excellent." Tawny claps, rushing ahead of us. "I'll get it all set up."

Cody's lips hook into a gloating smile, and I'm beginning to feel like I'm the one that just got *set up*.

CHAPTER
FOURTEEN

JENNA

I GLANCE down at my phone, disregarding the extra skip in my heartbeat from seeing Cody's name on my screen.

Cody: Are you ready to show everyone how much you love and adore me?

Jenna: If you mean, am I ready to tackle the hardest acting role of my life, then yes.

I smile as I send off the text.

Cody: It's only the hardest acting role of your life because you haven't had that many yet.

Jenna: No, it's the hardest acting role because it involves pretending to be in a real relationship with you.

Cody: You know, I'm wildly turned on by sassiness in a woman.

I wasn't trying to be sassy. I was actually being honest.

Jenna: Unfortunately, I think you're wildly turned on by anything a woman does.

He sends me a winking emoji before his next text pops up. This feels like flirting.

Why am I text-flirting with Cody? There aren't any cameras or anyone here to witness our back-and-forth conversation. I should be in off mode.

Cody: So, should I stop by your room to pick you up?

Terrible idea—complete red flag for my heart.

Jenna: How about I meet you outside by the car?

Cody: What if somebody sees us walking out? Isn't the point of this brunch for us to be together?

I tighten my jaw, hating that he's right. It's important that the employees at the bed and breakfast where we're staying during filming believe that we're a couple. Any half-decent tabloid journalist will do some digging around here in Canada.

Cody: Plus, you said after the interview yesterday that we need to convince people that we're crazy about each other.

Jenna: Stop quoting me. It's annoying.

Cody: Stop saying things that should be quoted.

He bugs me. Like, a lot. I'm bothered by Cody Banner *a lot.*

Jenna: Room 17.

Cody: Thank you. I'll be there shortly.

He sends me a kissy emoji.

This is bad.

My mind races with the last time Cody stopped by my room, and I wince.

It was almost a week ago in Malibu.

Don't go there. DON'T GO THERE!

Dang. I went there.

Visions of Cody shirtless with his well-defined hip muscles roll through my head, like a kid somersaulting down a steep hill. And in that vision, he pins me with his smoldering blue eyes while whispering, "I think you're a beautiful woman, and I'm attracted to you too."

What the heck, Jenna!

My thoughts sound like a bodice-ripping romance novel. Starting off this brunch in the right headspace, are we?

I point at myself in the mirror. "You will get your shiz together right now if it kills you. None of this *oh-he's-so-handsome-how-can-I-resist-him* crap. You're in charge." I point at myself again in the mirror. "Take control of the situation. Turn it on, and then turn it right back off again. You are more efficient than the Clapper Lights. Clap it on, then clap it off!"

A heavy knock hits the door.

Pointing at the mirror one last time, I shoot a warning glare at myself before greeting him.

I yank the door open. Immediately, my gaze sweeps over his perfectly trimmed beard and broad shoulders, then to his well-worked-out arms and—

Nope!

My mind does a double clap, shutting off that prohibited activity. Checking Cody out is not allowed.

He peeks around me. "Is someone here? I thought I heard talking."

"Television," I quickly say, pulling the door shut behind me.

"I don't have a TV in my room."

Nice, Jenna. You don't have a TV either.

I blow a raspberry, adding a shrug. "I guess that tells you who they consider the more famous celebrity."

Cody shoots me his amused smile. "I guess so."

"Should we go?"

He gestures for me to walk first, but as soon as I forge ahead, I feel his hand on my lower back, guiding me.

I pause my steps, glancing over my shoulder. Cody didn't anticipate the abrupt stop, and by the time he does, he's so close to me that his chest presses against my back, and the soft touch of his hand has now turned into two hands cupping both sides of my hips in order to steady himself so he doesn't completely run me over.

The tip of my nose brushes the dark hair on his jaw, and my eyes slowly glance upward to meet his. "What do you think you're doing?"

"I was attempting to walk."

"I mean, what do you think you're doing with your hands?" I drop my chin, nodding in the direction of my hips, but the action puts his hot breath and lips grazing over the delicate spot between my eyebrow and the corner of my eye. A blast of delicious sensitivity flames over my skin. I reluctantly lift my head, finding his gaze again.

His eyes skewer me. "I wasn't aware I couldn't touch you. There are no rules."

Rules: the one thing Cody is hung up on and the exact thing Trey said to avoid.

"The contract doesn't spell out any specifics," he continues. "So if you don't want my hands on your body, you'll have to tell me." The close proximity of his words sends goosebumps tracking over each dip of my spine.

The more Cody tries to fish rules out of me, the more stubborn I become. Rules are a bad idea, especially with a playboy. They'd become a game to him, something to obliterate and conquer. I've seen it in books and movies a hundred times before. You set rules, practically begging yourself to break them. That's not happening here. We're not setting lines just to cross them, or coming up with rules just to break them.

No rules. No problems.

"For someone who likes to memorize everything I say, I'm surprised you still need clarification. There are no rules."

"You seem like the type of person who would normally like rules."

He's got me there. I love rules, guidelines, instructions—pretty much anything I can follow—but not in this situation. With Cody, I need to act like I don't care, like this entire fake relationship means nothing. I'm completely unaffected by him.

I laugh, showing how much I don't care. "You only make rules if you have something to protect or something you don't want to lose."

His brows raise. "And you think we don't?"

I'm bluffing. I'm trying to protect my heart because I definitely don't want to lose it to him.

Be confident.

Be bold.

Be brave.

That sounds like something that should be written on a t-shirt, not the mantra for my fake relationship. Maybe after all this with Cody, I can sell shirts with that saying on Etsy—make millions.

My chin lifts, checking off the confident and bold categories of my t-shirt business/fake relationship slogan. "This isn't real, so therefore, we have nothing to lose. We're just acting." I move to step away from him since I think we've been smooshed together long enough.

"Not so fast." Both hands grab at my waist, and as if we're professional ballroom dancers, Cody effortlessly spins me around so I'm facing him chest to chest. His flirty smile kills me, adding to the perpetual beats of my heart.

"You should probably save the PDA for when we really need it. I'd hate for you to tire out early." I reach for my hips, thinking I can somehow remove his hands, but instead, my fingers tangle together with his. So now we're face to face, his hands holding me to him, my hands on top of his, his heartbeat pounding through his chest to mine, and his sultry blue eyes piercing me.

My breaths are patchy and frazzled, and my resolve to pretend that this thing between us doesn't matter and isn't killing me starts to slip. It shouldn't be this hard to keep real feelings gated in.

"Don't worry about me. I won't tire. I have plenty of stamina when it comes to this fake relationship."

"Your confidence is heart-warming, but let's just save the physical touch for when it's necessary."

"That sounds like a rule."

"More like a fake relationship unofficial motto."

"We don't have rules, but we have mottos?"

"*We* don't have anything, so you can let go of me now."

His brows lift as his gaze bounces behind me. I turn my head, and sure enough, there's a couple down the hall, gawking. The wife has her phone out like she's about to take a picture of us, or maybe she just did. I remind myself of all the reasons why I need this fake relationship to be believable: it will help my career, it will help the show, it will give hundreds of people jobs, and it will help ratings so season two can get signed. And with those reasons at the tip of my brain, I clap it *on.*

My arms lift, circling around Cody's neck, hugging him to me even more. There's a spark of surprise in his eyes, like he wasn't expecting me to play along, but that lasts only a moment before he smirks in one of his too-handsome-for-his-own-good kind of ways. I'm matching him stride for stride, so I tip my lips into a smile I'm sure I've never used on him before. Our gazes hold as I slowly shift my head to the side until the last second when my eyelids hover closed, and I softly kiss his cheek, his jawline, and his neck. Honestly, with Cody's short beard, who knows how much he actually feels of the action—probably nothing. But I *feel* a lot. I feel his strong arms wrapped around my waist, spurts of warm breath on my neck, the roughness of his beard against my skin.

And the smell.

Holy moly, the smell.

It's soap, but not the same low-budget crap that's in my room's shower and will never be given the chance to grace my skin and body. It's like the manliest-smelling soap I've ever encountered, with subtle hints of spice, or pine, or I don't even know. But I'm willing to spend an afternoon at a soap factory and sniff all the samples until I discover what it is that makes his scent so completely intoxicating.

"You smell good too," he whispers into the crook of my neck.

My body stiffens.

Did Cody hear me *sniff* him? Repeatedly? Feel my nose trail around the base of his neck like some kind of scent hound hunting its prey?

There's nothing embarrassing about that at all.

Nothing.

"I didn't even notice your scent." I pull away, brushing my hair back from my face. "Do you smell good?" I lean forward, dramatically making a show of smelling him. I hold my nose there, shaking my head. "I don't smell anything. But thank you for saying I smell good." I glance behind at the clear hallway, wondering how long we've actually been alone. "We should go."

I flip my gaze back to Cody. There's amusement in his eyes. So much amusement.

"Let's go, then."

I untangle from his arms and speed-walk down the 1986-inspired hallway to the stairs.

This is me clapping off.

CHAPTER
FIFTEEN

CODY

I WALK around the rental car, opening Jenna's door for her. Two photographers line up on the street in front of the cafe as if they knew exactly where we'd be and when.

Tawny and Dallas clearly know what they're doing.

The closest town to where we're filming is Banff, a picturesque national park, hopping with travelers. It's the perfect place for a sighting of the new Hollywood *It* couple. When tourists see the paparazzi taking our pictures, the sidewalk crowds with people trying to get a glimpse of someone famous.

There's a line of spectators on either side as I help Jenna out of the car. She eyes my proffered hand.

"You're crazy about me, remember?"

Her lips purse. Since when did lip pursing become so sexy? I don't know, but I'm a fan.

I pull her to a stand, thinking I'll lead her through the tunnel of people calling our names. But instead of heading straight for the door, Jenna stops and begins greeting the fans. She smiles for pictures and signs autographs on paper that literally came from out of nowhere.

"Cody, come be in this picture with us." She waves me over.

I'm not the best with fan interaction. I like to remain mysterious, which is really code for *distant*. But Jenna waves me over again, and I gravitate toward her. She puts her arm around me, smiling up at the phone.

"Oh, no!" She laughs with the woman who posed with us. "I think I closed my eyes. We need to take another."

Not only does she have time for one picture, but apparently, Jenna has time for two pictures. I guess this is how you become likable.

"Cody"—she waves me over again to a new fan—"this is Blake. He's a huge fan of yours."

She found that out in the two seconds she spent with him?

The little boy looks up at me with a toothless grin. "*Defend or Die* is my favorite movie."

"*Defend or Die*? Really? Aren't you a little too young to be watching an action movie like that?" Jenna swats my shoulder. "What I meant to say is, I'm so glad you liked it."

We continue this sort of thing all the way down the line of fans—me hanging back while Jenna effortlessly connects to people in a way I've only ever dreamed about. At the end, the restaurant hostess sees us coming and promptly opens the door.

"Welcome to Mont Cafe," she says. "We have a table waiting for you on the patio."

"The patio?" Jenna asks. "That sounds quaint."

I wink at her. "Only the best for my baby bumpkins."

"So now I'm a *baby* bumpkins?"

"I'm just feeling out all my options."

Her eye roll makes it seem like she's over my teasing, but I see how she's biting back a smile.

We follow the hostess to our spot at the edge of the patio. There's a slight breeze, but beyond that, the summer air is perfect for sitting outside. We're seated beside the two-foot privacy fence that separates where the sidewalk stops and the cafe begins. Each table has a canopy overhead, blocking the morning sun with mountain views on all sides. It would be ideal if it weren't for the crowd of people twenty feet away, holding phones to take pictures of us. Luckily, the cafe enforces that they can't come right to where we're seated.

I help Jenna into her chair, and we smile politely as the hostess places our napkins in our laps like we can't do it ourselves.

"Your waiter will be with you shortly."

"Thanks." I wait a second for her to clear before turning to Jenna with a teasing grin. "Should we hold hands across the table? Start off with a bang?"

She keeps her hands firmly in her lap. "Is that how you do it with all your dates?"

"Are you implying I date a lot of women?"

"Yes."

Her words don't hurt my feelings, but there is a want—or maybe it's a *need*—for her to know the truth. So I lay the fake relationship aside for a minute and start with honesty.

"It's not true."

She takes a sip of her water. "What's not true?"

"All the women."

She gives me a pointed stare, letting me know she doesn't believe a word I'm saying.

"Okay, fine. It used to be true." I bounce my head back and forth. "Five or six years ago, maybe, but not since then."

Jenna's brows lift in interest. "You're telling me you haven't dated anyone for six years?"

"Maybe three or four." I smile.

"Is that number going to keep going down the more we talk? By the end of the meal, will it come out that it's only been a week since you had your last fling?"

"Well, I did spend a steamy weekend in Malibu with one girl, but I don't think she likes me too much."

"I don't think she likes being one of *many* women."

"Then she should know that three years ago was my last fling. Final answer."

She stares back at me, a vivid war playing across her face.

"Is that true?" She leans forward, resting her elbows on the table.

"Yes."

"I saw you talk on the phone to Calista James for almost forty-five minutes the other night."

"A friendly conversation with a friend." I debate offering up more information than that, giving Jenna the complete rundown of Calista's and my friendship and how, somewhere along the way, I became her confidant, but I decide those kinds of details don't matter. We're friends. Jenna already knows what friendships look like.

"So you're saying you haven't dated anyone for three years. That's a long time for a man like you."

"I'm going to pretend you mean that in the best way possible and not take offense." She sniffs out a laugh. "But so you know, for the last three years, I've focused on work. I've been filming four movies a year plus squeezing in promoting them. I've been too busy to think about that kind of stuff."

"Then why are you rumored to be with a new woman every month?"

"I told you in Malibu. That's the only thing the media wants to talk about when it comes to me. Juicy gossip sells better than my acting does."

"That's not true. Your acting sells."

"I could deliver the best role of my life, win every single award, and the headlines would still be about what woman I took home with me that weekend. But it's fine. I've had the playboy label so long that I'm used to it. And it probably is a better story than my acting skills."

"Do you think you're a good actor?"

"Sometimes."

"Only sometimes?"

I shrug.

"I think you're a good actor." She hesitates for a second. "No, actually, I think you're a *great* actor."

I can't help the huge smile her words have smeared across my face, even if I don't believe they're true. "Oh, come on. You're just saying that because you think I was fishing for a compliment."

"No, really. I've learned so much from you these last few months. Take that scene in the garden we filmed the other night. You portrayed so much longing and sadness in your work. It was really impressive."

That's because I wasn't acting.

"You have this natural ability to take a character or a scene and make it your own, whereas I have a hard time letting myself go and just immersing myself in the story. I can see why you've been so frustrated with me."

"I've only been frustrated with you because I don't understand you."

"I know." She takes another sip of her water. "My methods of going over and over a scene don't make any sense."

"That's not what I mean." I keep my gaze on Jenna, waiting for her eyes to meet mine. "I don't understand how to get you to like me or how to draw that same genuine smile out of you that you give other people. I can eventually win people over with my teasing and charisma, but not you. You're baffling."

Her lips loosen into a smirk—something she rarely gives me. "I'm not that baffling."

"Yes, you are. I'm constantly wondering what you think of me." I lean forward, resting my weight on my folded arms, matching Jenna's position. The round table between us is small enough that our faces are only six inches apart. "I probably should've asked when we were playing twenty questions. I could've disguised my curiosity under something like, *what was your first impression of me?*"

Her smirk slowly turns into a small-scale smile. "I thought you were cocky and arrogant in the charming kind of way that no woman can resist."

The corner of my mouth lifts higher. "But you can resist."

"I can resist." She nods, and with any other woman, I would swear she was flirting with me, but with Jenna, I'm unsure. "And what about me? What was your first impression of me?"

"You frustrated me because you'd already decided you didn't like me and wouldn't even give me the time of day."

"Of course I didn't like you. You couldn't even remember who I was."

"I'm not talking about the side of the road. I'm talking about that night eight years ago when we met in the bathroom."

"I thought you didn't count that as officially meeting."

"Do you really think I'd forget an encounter with a smart and bossy woman in a sparkly black dress with a low V in front and in back?"

Her eyes light with surprise. "You thought I was smart?"

"I remember you talked circles around me that night, and I believe you tried to figure out the blood-alcohol level of the poor drunk girl. It was cute, and although it was brief, I liked how you kept me on my toes. Still do."

She flashes me a different kind of smile, bracketed by a slight blush dotting both cheeks. The reaction makes me think no one has ever complimented her on anything other than her looks.

A slight breeze swirls around us, picking up a strand of Jenna's hair and blowing it over her part. I slowly reach my arm out, keeping my gaze on her the entire time. She doesn't move, just watches me with her vibrant green eyes as my fingers comb through the stray piece and tuck it behind her ear.

There's a spark between us. The unexplainable chemistry that was missing during filming has flickered to life in the middle of a cafe in Banff.

"What can I get you two to drink?" The waiter beside our table completely ruins the moment.

"Uh." Jenna shakes her head, sitting back in her chair, making the small table feel like a million miles of unwanted space. "I'll just have water."

"And for you?"

"Water is great."

"Are you ready to order?"

I grab the menus in front of us, that we haven't even looked at yet, and hand one to Jenna. "No, we're going to need another minute."

He turns and leaves, but I've lost Jenna. Her nose is deep in the menu.

"It all looks so good," she muses.

"Yeah." I glance down, not really seeing the words. Instead, I'm wondering how I can rewind things back to how they were thirty seconds ago.

Jenna's cell phone rings, and she quickly digs it out of her purse. My eyes shoot to the name on the screen as she swipes the call open.

Dave.

No last name.

Just Dave.

"Oh, shoot. I have to take this." She scoots her chair back, waving to me. "Just order me whatever you're having."

Her back turns as she walks away, but I still hear the overly enthusiastic way she says, "Dave!" as she answers the phone.

She implied the other night, while filming the garden scene, that she didn't have a boyfriend. But the mysterious Dave seems awfully suspicious. Maybe it's not serious. Or maybe it is. I take a drink of my water, because suddenly everything feels tight and hot.

Jenna walks to the other side of the patio. She's smiling—like, really big—as she talks on the phone, and by the time she gets back to the table, I'm convinced this Dave guy has just proposed, and she gladly said yes.

"Sorry about that." She sits back down.

"No worries." Except for the fact that you just got engaged while on a date with me. "Is everything okay?" I'm perfectly collected, despite the devastating news.

"Yes!" Her eyes beam with happiness. "It's more than okay."

Here comes a description of the three-carat diamond that Dave bought from Tiffany's.

"That was my friend, Dave."

Friend. Okay. Thanks for the clarification.

"He has this amazing non-profit organization that travels all over the world to underprivileged countries where people live in these remote villages, and they don't have clean water, or good medical treatment, or school supplies. And he basically brings in an entire team of people to help dig wells and trenches, or build hospitals, or make repairs on existing houses. It's just great what he does, and as soon as he told me, I knew I wanted to be involved. I'm just so passionate about what he's doing." If the bright, glimmering sparkle in her eyes is any indication of her passion, then I believe it. "He was calling to let me know that the trip we've been planning for next spring just got approved. I'm so excited to finally see my money going to a good cause and making a difference."

Her smile widens in that genuine way I've come to adore, and my heart aches. It literally aches because of Jenna's uninhibited goodness. I've never cared about being deserving of a woman like her until now.

"That's awesome," I manage between thoughts of how I need to change pretty much everything about myself so I can become more like her.

"Yeah, it is." She self-consciously tucks her hair behind her ear. "But anyway, I don't want to bore you with that."

"I'm not bored."

Her lips softly press into a smile. "You're not?"

"Not at all. I want to hear all about it. Tell me everything."

Because if Jenna is passionate about it, it's definitely worth knowing.

JENNA

THIS FEELS LIKE A DATE—AND not a fake date.

A *first* date.

A really, really good first date with a man who's actually interested in me for me, which never happens—like ever. There's talking and getting to know each other and laughter and amazing conversation. Who knew Cody was capable of all that?

I, for sure, did not.

But I'm not supposed to be enjoying my time with him. I'm supposed to be making people think we're the most in-love Hollywood couple there ever was—Ryan Reynolds and Blake Lively status. And if we don't deliver that kind of performance, Tawny and Dallas will make us repeat this whole thing again, which I don't know if I can handle.

Actually, it's the sweet, vulnerable side of Cody that I can't handle. Things were much easier when I thought he was just some sleazy playboy going from one woman to the next. But maybe I misjudged him. Because what I see in front of me is a man who just wants to be liked for all the right reasons and none of the wrong—basically the story of my life. He's attentive, and funny, and isn't trying to impress me with talk about himself. Our conversations have mostly been about me and my interests, which is a nice change for once.

"Here's your check," the waiter says, dropping a paper face down on the table.

"I got it." Cody picks it up before I have the chance.

"At least let me pay my half."

"Call me old-fashioned, but I believe a man should take care of his woman."

His woman?

I'm skating past that as if I were Michelle Kwan herself, because I'm not really his woman. I'm just some girl he has to pretend to be interested in to boost his career.

"I see how you work," I joke as the waiter walks away with his card. "You just want credit with the paparazzi for paying."

Cody turns his head to the side as if he'd forgotten about the watching crowd of people twenty feet away. "I don't care about them."

"You should." My eyes follow his. "Do you think we've done enough to convince them we're in love?"

"Nope."

"Really?" I don't know why I'm acting so surprised. The only time we touched was when Cody fixed my hair. The simple action made my heart feel like it was pumping lava instead of blood—probably why I haven't attempted any physical contact of my own.

I don't trust my body not to react.

"We're not even close to convincing them," he says.

"Not even close?"

"Nope."

"So what do we need to do, then?"

"That depends."

"On what?"

"On how committed you are to selling this story." His expression changes from normal to heated instantly. "Because if you're committed, there are a lot of ways I can convince them."

I blame the pounding in my heart for my next words. "Show me."

Cody's blue eyes lock on me. "First of all, we're sitting way too far apart." He casually scoots his chair over, resting his arm on the back of mine, gently rubbing his thumb along my shoulder blade as he talks.

"Distance is important," I mumble.

We're right next to each other now, awkwardly gazing into each other's eyes, but I can't look away because I don't want to miss a single one of his slow, sexy movements. It's the way he rolled up next to me, right in my space, with all the confidence in the world.

And that stare.

Cody Banner knows how to kill a woman with the intensity of his stare. I've literally died all the deaths from his smoldering gaze.

"Then what?" Somewhere in the back of my mind, an angel shakes her head at my complete lack of self-control. She might also be yelling, '*Why are you encouraging this stupid game?!*'

For the series.

For the ratings.

For my job.

For my mantra.

For anything other than my own desires.

I'm innocent—a lie I'll keep telling myself because it sounds so good.

Cody brushes my hair off my shoulder, clearing a path to my neck. "For best optics, I'd live right here." His nose slowly skims over my jawline, down my neck to my collarbone, stopping at my ear. It's the same action I did to him in the hall back at the bed and breakfast, and let me tell you, it's an effective strategy. My stomach flips and bounces around. I'm seriously wondering if I was born with all the correct gastrointestinal parts, because there's so much stomach flipping happening. Like, shouldn't a small intestine stop some of that movement? If not the small, at least the large.

"And we can't forget about hand holding."

"Hand holding is good." Somehow, repeating his words keeps me grounded in this moment. Otherwise, I might drift away, lost on cloud nine forever.

Cody's fingers trail from the tip of my shoulder to my wrist until they lock together with mine. My eyes drop to his forearm and the sexy way his veins twist and move as he intertwines our hands. Why are big veins on a man's arm so *manly*? I don't know. But I bet nurses would line up for miles for a chance to give Cody and his big sexy veins an IV.

"But that's just a start," he whispers against my ear. My breath purposely stills so I can focus on his touch. I can't be bothered with breathing right now. I'm fixated on each sweet sensation from his grazes. I feel the brush of his lips and beard against the soft shell, and now all I can think about is how much I wish he'd press a gentle kiss to my ear, or my cheek, or anywhere in that vicinity. I've reached an all-time low by having a mid-morning fantasy in a cafe in public, but I'm not even embarrassed. Carry on, my friend. Carry on.

"There'd be no stopping me from kissing you," Cody whispers, "if this were real."

My eyes pop open—I didn't even register that they were closed—and drift to Cody.

"But it's not real," I say more to myself than to him.

"No, it's not real."

Our stares hold strong until the waiter comes back with his credit card.

"Thank you for coming." He places it on the table, and we

both use the interruption as a way to casually break apart from each other without it looking bad for the cameras.

But the damage has already been done.

I mixed fiction with reality.

Well done, Jenna.

Well done.

CHAPTER
SIXTEEN

CODY

"THESE PHOTOGRAPHS from your brunch yesterday are pretty convincing." Dallas sits beside me in a director's chair, scrolling through his phone. "And I'm not even talking about the ones where you and Jenna were touching. Those were flamin', by the way." I look at Mr. L.L. Bean and shake my head, wishing he would never use the word *flamin'* in the same sentence as me. It's just weird. "I'm talking about the ones where you two were photographed conversing. I mean, even those are scorchin'."

Heat synonyms must be a thing with him today.

"Let me see the pictures." I lean over, looking at Dallas's phone.

It's odd seeing a snapshot of the moment. Playing it back in my mind, I told myself Jenna was just enduring her time with me until brunch was over, but the photographs tell a different story. She looks happy, like she was enjoying herself. It's hard to believe a woman as incredible as Jenna could enjoy herself with me, but pictures don't lie.

Unless she was acting. Then pictures could lie.

"And look at the headline." Dallas points to his screen,

reading aloud as if I'm four. "Has Jenna Lewis finally tamed the bad boy? Sources say yes." His eyes swing to me excitedly. "Didn't I say this whole charade would be perfect for your image?"

"Yeah." My gaze drifts to Jenna across the field. She steals the show in a maroon dress, pleated in the front, nipping everything together at her waist in a flattering way. Her golden hair weaves in and out in an intricate braid, falling over one shoulder—she has to be the makeup and costume teams' dream come true.

I wish we filmed together today, but instead, we've been doing other scenes, and it sucks.

Teague stands by her, laughing as they watch footage from the scene they just filmed of Drake and Renna in the bathroom. I've never been more grateful that Teague is married and not a romantic option for Jenna. His good-boy charm would completely outshine me if he were available. That type of thing, along with goodness and wholesomeness, is probably right up her alley.

I turn to Dallas. "What do you know about Jenna's past relationships?"

He doesn't even look up from his phone. "What do you mean?"

"Like, who has she dated in the past?"

"I don't know. Did you Google it?"

"No."

Dallas's eyes finally lift. "Why not?"

"Because Google is not the most reliable source when it comes to celebrities' dating history. Take me, for example."

"Why do you want to know?"

I can't tell him it's because I want to see how far away from Jenna's type I am.

"I don't know. Just curious." I tack on a shrug for added indifference. "I thought you might know since you work in publicity."

"I honestly haven't paid attention." His gaze goes back to his phone, and mine goes back to Jenna.

We sit silently for a few minutes while I watch her until, finally, I say, "Hey, Dallas?"

"Yeah?"

"I was thinking I might consider donating to a charity or something."

"That's a great idea." All his focus is on me now. "We could get pictures of you donating a check or playing with sick kids. You'd look like you have a heart of gold."

I don't want to *look* like I have a heart of gold. I actually want to have a heart of gold. There's a big difference. Something I'm learning the hard way.

"This isn't a publicity stunt. I don't want anyone to know about it."

"Why do it, then?"

"Because I want to help troubled teens whose parents are in custody battles."

"I can get you lined up with a charity more important than that."

That's always been the problem. Nobody looks after these kinds of kids—kids like me. There's always someone or something else that's a worthier cause. But not to me.

I shake my head. "I don't want something more important. I'm passionate about the custody battle thing."

Dallas's brows drop. "Custody battles?"

"Yeah."

"I'll see what I can find out."

"Thanks."

I'm taking a page from Jenna's book and looking outward instead of inward. And, who knows? Maybe I can help a kid whose life is messed up because they're caught in a custody battle and don't know where to turn or who to trust. Just one person who cared about me when I was a teenager would've made a big difference.

"But I still think we should use the charity as a way to add credibility to your rising image."

"Not this time."

"I know you don't believe that I'm doing anything, but I got you this far, didn't I?" He shoots me a sly smile that doesn't sit well.

"What do you mean?"

"You think that a random photographer just happened to be on the beach in Malibu near the exact house you and Jenna were staying at?"

Pieces start to fit together. "You did this?"

"Of course I did. Tawny likes to take credit for everything, but this fake relationship was all me. I told you a decoy relationship with a good girl was the way to go."

"Dallas." My eyes narrow on him.

"What? You hired me to do a job, and I'm doing it."

"Yeah, but Jenna thinks those pictures were taken at random. She'll feel completely blindsided if she knows we were set up."

"She's not going to care when she sees all the ways this fake relationship benefits her career."

"I don't like it."

"Oh, please. Just say thank you and be on your way."

I guess, in a small way, I am thankful. Not for the boost in my likability, but for the extra time this whole ruse gets me with Jenna.

Dallas Mikesell might just be worth every single penny I pay him.

I STARE at a blank Google screen on my laptop as I lie in bed that night. Do I really want to know all the men Jenna has dated in the past? It's probably a long list of Nobel Prize winners or a relative of Mother Teresa—things I'm never going to be able to measure up to. But I type out the words anyway and hit return.

The page instantly fills with information, and against my better judgment, I click on the first link that says: Jenna Lewis Dating History.

I start at the beginning, when she was just nineteen years old and new to modeling. Rand Phillipe was a British photographer ten years older than Jenna. My jaw clenches with each picture of them together, not because she's with another man but because, in every shot, he's either walking one step ahead of her, has his back to her, or isn't paying any attention to her. I'm surprised she lasted seven months with the jerk.

Next was a professional football player and teammate to her brother, Nixon Porter. They dated for three months when she was twenty-one, with few pictures or information about the relationship.

Then comes a long line of men over the last five years: musicians, actors, professional hockey players, businessmen. The tabloid gossip—if you can even believe any of it—has most of them cheating on or breaking up with her. There's even a meme of the last guy she dated—some sports agent who was photographed looking jealous over another woman when he was supposed to be dating Jenna.

What a jerk.

That's when it hits me.

I'm exactly like all of these men Jenna has dated, and it makes me sad because I want better than that for her, better than *me*. Not that I've ever been in the running for her heart or ever would be, but neither should these guys. She deserves so much more than what she's settled for in the past, and I want to make sure she realizes that.

I'll be the best fake boyfriend there ever was.

CHAPTER
SEVENTEEN

JENNA

"SCENE 33D." The camera assistant holds the sticks in front of the camera and claps the slate together as she yells, "Take five."

Quinton shifts in his seat from the director's chair. "Action!"

Cody descends the large staircase while I climb it, holding the railing for dear life. Each step is carefully placed since I tripped on my dress the first five takes. After the last time, wardrobe came and tucked and pinned what they could to shorten the length. Hopefully, I can walk without tripping now. It's not my fault. The hem on my yellow dress was longer than Rihanna's train at the Met Gala in 2015 and 2023—the woman loves trailing fabric. But even though we've been filming for months, I still feel like a beginner. Like everyone is judging me or critiquing me. Right now, there are probably a dozen crew members wondering how I ever made it down a runway when I can't even make it up this giant staircase.

But then I look at Cody, and he's all smiles and softness, and suddenly my insecurities vanish.

He stops mid-staircase and grins like Trev would at Renna in *The Promised Prince*. "You missed the fireworks last night."

I glance away from him, channeling Renna's hurt and pain. "I saw them," I deliver my line with an edge.

"Oh, I thought I saw you leave with Drake."

"I did leave the fireworks display." My mind flashes to a vision of my notes from this scene and the highlighted stage cue to fold my arms. I cut my gaze to Cody and cross my arms over my chest. "But I saw the ones later that night."

Cody feigns confusion. "What fireworks? I don't understand."

"You know, the ones between you and Seran in the royal living room."

We filmed that yesterday, and to be honest, I'm surprised by how little acting I needed to do for that scene. Watching Cody kiss Kylee Truro, who plays Seran, was like a punch to the gut over and over again. I think we did thirteen takes of that scene to get all the different camera angles. That's thirteen times Cody had to kiss Kylee. I know it's fake and acting, and there's absolutely nothing romantic about having so many people hover and watch, but still, their kisses put twisty, jealous feelings in my stomach.

In that moment, I really did feel like my character, Renna Degray, making it easy to draw upon those jealous feelings for this scene too.

I wait for Cody to say his line, then harden my jaw as I deliver mine. "Your kiss with Seran."

"You saw that?"

"I wasn't spying or anything. I just wanted to tell you something, but you were"—I press my lips into a tight smile just like the script choreographed—"*busy*, and I didn't want to interrupt your intimate moment."

In real life, I totally wanted to interrupt Cody and Kylee's intimate moment. *Moments*—thirteen of them, to be exact. I wanted to yell, 'CUT!' or, 'That's a wrap!' but no.

Camera angles and lighting took precedence over my feelings.

But it's fine.

The jealousy was a small lapse in judgment, a time when I let my character's feelings intermingle with my own. I mean, I don't even like Cody, so why do I care if he kisses a stunning brunette with full lips and dark eyes?

"It wasn't an intimate moment," Cody—er, Trev—says.

Ha! I want to roll my eyes, but I don't because I don't care.

And neither does Renna Degray. So I pull my shoulders back and answer for the both of us. "It looked pretty intimate to me. Anyway, I'm happy for you both." I lift my chin and slip past Cody, continuing my ascent up the stairs, mindful, as always, not to trip on my dress.

"Renna?" Cody touches my arm, and my skin zings. It *zings!*

It's been two days since our fake brunch, since I felt the warmth of his fingers on me, and I'd be lying if I said I didn't miss this feeling.

Wish for it.

Desire it.

Crave it.

I'm like an addict who needs her fix.

Cody's eyes lock on mine, and his lips tilt. My heartbeat builds, and all I can think about is staying in this feeling, in this *zing,* for as long as possible.

That's why I don't immediately pull away like I'm supposed to—like Renna needs to.

"Jenna," Quinton says, circling his fingers around, "let's do it again, but this time, immediately pull away when Cody grabs your arm. Stay there for his last few lines, then once you say yours, turn and go."

I drop my arm, nodding as I go back to the original step I started on. Everyone repositions, and I start again with my last line and then begin walking up the steps.

"Renna?" Cody says, reaching for me, but I reluctantly pull away this time.

"I'm really busy. I have to go." I force detachment into my voice even though the last thing I want right now is to be detached from Cody, but I focus as he finishes his monologue, pushing a giant smile on my face like Renna would.

"I'm not hurt." I shake my head with my fake smile. "Like I said, I'm happy for you." I turn and rush up the stairs until Quinton says cut.

The watching crew members clap.

"Nicely done!" Quinton hops out of his chair, running up the steps to where I meet him and Cody in the middle. He shakes his head as he laughs. "I don't know what happened, but whatever it is, don't change a thing. Chemistry and angst drip off of you two in droves. I love it! I love it!"

"You know what they say..."—Cody smirks—"fighters make the best lovers." His eyes catch mine, and we exchange a look, a shared feeling that I'm not admitting or acknowledging.

"Well, it's definitely true for the both of you." Quinton pats us on the shoulders before marching down the stairs. "Let's reset and take it from the top. But first, play back the footage so I can see the angles."

"Do you want to go watch the playback?" I gesture down to the camera.

"I don't think we need to." He steps onto the stair just below where I'm standing, putting our bodies a few inches apart. His smile is easy, and his eyes bounce with playfulness or flirtiness, some kind of -ness that has my heart racing. "You heard Quinton. Chemistry and angst drip off us in droves." Cody's hand on the banister inches toward mine until the tips brush against my fingers.

And oh my lanta!

I don't even know what a *lanta* is, but Cody's simple touch has it ohhing.

"I thought angst was bad," I say, leaning toward him. "Do we really want that coming off us in droves?"

"It's not always bad. Angst can imply uneasiness caused by tension and buildup." Now it's his turn to lean and move forward.

"Good tension?" I lift my brows and stretch my fingers, feeling more of his hand.

"The best kind." His words are soft and secretive, like he doesn't want anyone else to share in this moment with us.

I smile in reaction. "Too much tension can be bad if you let it build up too long."

"Jenna? Cody?" Quinton waves us down to the camera. "I want you to come see this."

Cody turns to me with a charged smile that makes my stomach swoop. He leans forward, hovering his lips just above my ear. "Nah, buildup is the best part."

My breath hitches as he backs away. He takes the steps two at a time until he's at the bottom. I don't move for a second. All I can think about is how he's right.

The buildup *is* the best part.

I follow after him, blushing the entire way down.

CHAPTER
EIGHTEEN

CODY

WE TAKE a break from filming to eat while the cameras and the lighting are moved to the next shooting spot on the property. As I make my way through the catered buffet line, my plate gets heavier with each item I dish onto it. At the end, I grab a water bottle before stopping to look for where Jenna is.

She's seated next to Tawny, but the other seat beside her is free.

I walk to them, hitting the back of the chair with my water bottle. "Is this spot open?"

Jenna glances at me with a smile. "Yeah, take a seat."

"Good." Tawny shuffles some papers in front of her. "I'm glad you're both here. There's something I want to discuss."

I'm not particularly glad Tawny is here. I would've preferred an intimate lunch alone with Jenna—something like our brunch two days ago. But honestly, any kind of intimacy with her is welcome.

Easy, buddy. This is all fake.

I sit, forcing myself to glance at Tawny and not Jenna. "What's up?"

Tawny laughs. "The show's ratings, for one." She holds up a paper like I can decipher numbers from across the table while eating a sandwich. "I mean, look at this." She points to the first line, and Jenna leans in to see. "That's where the ratings started after episode one aired last week." She points to another line. "And this number is where we're at today. Episode two came out at midnight last night, and one week of your fake relationship under our belts. I don't do math, but that's a huge increase."

"Yeah, it's a forty-two percent increase in ratings since the story broke that we're dating," Jenna says the number casually as she takes a bite of her salad.

Tawny's eyes light. "I'll leave the exact numbers to our master of accounting."

My eyes swing to Jenna. "Master of accounting?"

"Oh." Her gaze falls as if she's embarrassed. "I'm good with numbers."

"Good with numbers? Geez, girl. Give yourself more credit than that." Tawny hits her shoulder before flipping her stare to me. "Jenna graduated college with a Master's in Accounting."

"Wait." Brows dropping, I glance over at her. "You got your Master's in Accounting while working as a model?"

"Yeah." She shrugs. "I did most of it online."

"Are you serious? That's incredible."

"It's not that big of a deal."

"It is. I'm crazy impressed with you right now."

She laughs, shaking her head. "Don't be impressed. I'm kind of a nerd when it comes to numbers and accounting."

Tawny nods. "Yes, she's very smart. Now, can we move on to more important things?"

I sit back in my chair, unsure if I can move on. The more I get to know Jenna, the more amazed I become. And now I'm dying to learn everything about her so I can see the complete picture, because I have a feeling I've only scratched the surface of truly knowing her.

But instead of diving deep into Jenna, I'm stuck listening to Tawny's next idea of capitalizing on our fake love life.

"Jenna's brother is getting married next week, and I want you guys to attend together."

Jenna sits up at the same time I shake my head.

"Tawny, that's my brother's wedding. I'm not going to make Cody fly to Tampa and meet my family when this isn't a real relationship."

Taking Jenna's cue, I tack on more reasons why this isn't a good idea. "Yeah, that's a private family event. The Lewises don't need me hanging around."

Tawny's expression hardens. "This is non-negotiable. Nobody knows this whole thing is fake, and to keep it that way, you both need to attend the wedding together. It's a star-studded event. There will be photographers and paparazzi." Her eyes drift to Jenna. "What will everyone think if you show up at your brother's wedding without your boyfriend?" Jenna's shoulders drop as she thinks it through. "By then, filming will be done. You guys can leave from the wedding to go to LA and attend the wrap party together—another great place to solidify that you're a couple. These are the things we have to do until Flixmart picks up season two of the show."

"I guess you're right. Cody can come to the wedding." Jenna's gaze drifts to me. "As long as that's okay with you?"

"Only if you want me to come." Her nod is subtle, but it's enough. "Then I'll be there."

Is it bad that I was secretly hoping Jenna would want me there? Yeah, that's bad. I'm backpedaling now. "I mean, I'll come if Dallas is okay with it."

"Dallas!" Tawny scoffs. "You think he knows what's best? Pfft. I'm the mastermind here." She pulls a business card from her cleavage and holds it out to me. "Honey, when you're done with him, come on over. I'll show you what a real PR manager looks like."

"Did you just pull a business card out from your boobs?" Jenna tries to keep her amusement under wraps.

"I never leave home without one." She waves it in front of me again.

"Gee, thanks, Tawny." I take the card, trying not to notice the warm dampness that makes the stiff paper flimsier. "I'll be sure to hang onto this." I go to put it in my pocket, then remember, I'm in costume and only have fake pockets on my tailored pants.

"You do that, because when this relationship is over, I have several more clients we can set you up with. We'll have you likable in no time."

"Thanks, but I think one fake relationship is good enough for now."

Besides, I can't imagine going through this whole charade with anyone but Jenna.

CHAPTER
NINETEEN

JENNA

I'M RUNNING around my room at the bed and breakfast, trying to clean things up as fast as possible because Cody is coming over to watch episode two on my laptop.

With me.

In my room.

Alone.

At night.

All important details worth mentioning. I should also mention that this bed and breakfast was built in 1986. My room is small, and there isn't a couch or the expected mauve-and-baby-blue floral-wrapped chair. It's just the bed—and not even a queen-sized bed. It's a *full*.

So, me, Cody, and the full-sized bed.

No reason to panic.

This is like a business meeting. Coworkers go out to lunch. Costars watch romance shows in bed. No difference.

I glance at myself in the mirror. These daily pep talks have been critical in keeping my head in the right space.

"There will be absolutely no touching," I tell myself. "No meaningful conversations that make your heart feel soft and gooey. This is cut and dry. An analysis of our performance and what we can do better."

Two light taps shake the door.

I smooth my sweats, secretly wishing I hadn't told Winnie to only pack lame things, and then open the door.

"Heyyy," I drag out the word as if the slowness can somehow control the tempo of my racing heart.

"Hi." Cody's eyes sweep over me like a broom in a room with a lot of dust. Back and forth. Up and down. "You look really cute."

Cute.

Why is that the cutest thing any man has ever said to me? Probably because I'm used to other adjectives: hot, sexy, attractive, just to name a few. But there's something really sweet about being *cute.*

"Thanks, you look nice too."

"I'm in a t-shirt and sweats."

My eyes drop down my body. "So am I."

The tip of his finger lifts my chin so I'm looking directly into his blue eyes. "But you still look amazing." His hand drops as he moves past me into the room. "I'm glad your room smells old and musty like mine." He spins around. "I was starting to think it was me."

"No, I think it's from years and years of mildew."

His nose crinkles. "Gross."

"I thought if I became an actor, I'd be living a life of luxury, not be on the road all the time in old motel rooms or living out of trailers."

"It's not fancy, that's for sure."

We stare at each other for a few beats, trying to figure out how to transition into the next phase of the visit. But since I'm the host, it's up to me to pave the way.

"So," I gesture to the bed. "We'll have to watch the show here since there's no couch or anything else."

Cody nods, looking over the bed. "Sure, we'll each take a side."

He kicks off his shoes and sits on the edge while I grab my computer. It takes me a second, but I get Flixmart open and click on the show. The screen goes black except for a spinning circle in the middle.

"Maybe the Wi-Fi here can't support streaming, but we'll try it." I place the computer in the center of the bed and glance at Cody. We both lie back on separate sides, sticking our legs straight out. I'm stiff, like if I move even a centimeter, I'll somehow end up curled next to him.

He shifts his head, and I turn to look at him. "Can you see okay?" It's just the intro right now, but eventually, Cody will need to be able to see the screen comfortably.

His head angles toward me so it's more in the center of the bed. "That's better." Blue eyes flip to me. "What about you? Can you see?"

For some reason, I copy his position, angling my head toward him. We're like two sides of a triangle, our touching heads the point of intersection. "Uh, yeah. That's better."

We lie in silence, listening to the beautiful music and watching the rolling scenery as the opening credits flash onto the screen one at a time. Our hands are both clasped together, resting on each of our stomachs. A forklift could transfer me to a coffin, and I wouldn't have to move a muscle.

"This is a pretty song," Cody says.

"Yeah, they did a good job. Great use of instruments."

Great use of instruments?

If anyone else heard us, we'd lose all street cred for being Hollywood's biggest playboy and the sexiest woman alive. We're vanilla and not even the good-tasting kind. The bland vanilla that nobody likes.

"Are you nervous to see yourself?" I feel his head shift slightly, like he's trying to look at me, so I shift mine. Our eyes are millimeters apart, hot breaths mingling together between us.

"A little. Are you nervous?"

"A little."

We stare a second longer but turn our heads forward when the credits end and the opening scene begins.

The show starts with Cody storming through the castle to the training field. He removes his tie and jacket, looking for someone to fight him, until Teague steps in. They move back and forth and fall to the ground, wrestling.

I remember watching them film this scene. I learned a lot, paying attention to how they carried out fight choreography and movement. But what I don't remember about this scene is how dang good Cody looked in it. Because right now, all I can think about is his messed-up hair and heaving chest muscles.

"I feel stupid," he says, cutting into my daydream of how handsome and manly he is. His head shifts to me again. "It's awkward watching this together, isn't it?"

"It's not awkward." I gesture to the screen. "I was just thinking you did amazing in that scene." More like I thought you *looked* amazing. "There's no reason to feel awkward."

"Yeah, okay."

We keep watching, and now it's my turn to feel stupid. I'm with my maid getting ready for the welcome dinner that night, and all I want to do is cringe each time the camera zooms in on my face.

"Are we sure I'm a model? Because these up-close shots are brutal. You're right." I sigh. "It is awkward."

Both our heads turn toward each other at the same time. My gaze scans his handsome face, noting how trimmed and neat his short beard is. I've never dated a man with a beard before—stubble, yes, but a full beard is new for me. Not that Cody and I are dating…for real. I maintain that men like him have no place in my life, but that doesn't stop me from studying the dark-blue rim around his eyes.

"I don't know why it's awkward," Cody finally says.

"I don't know why either."

The talking in the background stops, and we glance at the screen. The show is stuck, buffering. But instead of pausing on some random thing, it's paused on my face mid-sentence. My eyes are big and wild, and some kind of double chin thing is happening. It's horrific—really, really ugly stuff.

I leap up, grasping for the computer, but two hands pull my waist, stopping my momentum. I yelp in surprise as I fall back onto the mattress, just as Cody dives forward. There's no way I'm letting him get control of that laptop and my ugly pause face, so I tackle him, wrapping my arms and legs around his body, trying to stop him.

"You really think you can take me?" he asks over his shoulder.

"My brother is a professional football player," I grunt as I hold him back. "I know a thing or two about wrestling."

"So do I." Cody is 6'2" and a million times stronger than me, so it's no surprise when he effortlessly flips me around and pins me on my back. He's not straddling me or even leaning over me closely—a shame, really—but we are in a playful stare-down as he holds my wrists on either side of me.

So much for not touching.

His beard frames his smile. "This feels a lot like episode one when we filmed Trev and Renna having a grass fight."

"Except, back then, we didn't know each other."

"How well do we really know each other now? I mean, you're some whiz kid accountant, and I didn't know that."

"What don't I know about you?" My eyes flit across his face, wondering how far I can push because I do want to know Cody better. I want to witness all the pieces that make him who he is. "When was the last time you saw your parents?"

His brows bunch together. "Are you trying to play twenty questions again?"

"If you'll let me."

He releases my hands and sits back, drawing in a deep breath. I slowly sit up, waiting for him to respond.

"My mom died three years ago. But before that, I'd only seen her a few times over the last twelve years."

"And your dad?" I gently press.

He threads his fingers through his dark hair, pushing it back from his face. "I saw him five years ago." His gaze lifts to mine. "He wanted money."

"Did you give it to him?"

"Nope."

"Why not?"

"Probably because I wanted to hurt him and then abandon him the way he did to me."

"So you're all alone?"

"It would appear so." The laughter that puffs over Cody's lips is more sad than humorous. "It's a funny thing being a celebrity or '*Hollywood's biggest hunk*.'" He lifts his fingers, putting the phrase in air quotes. "I'm so famous that no one would ever want to leave me. I'm too valuable. But at the same time, I don't add value. The fame has made me so unlikable that no one would ever want to stay with me." He shrugs, dropping his eyes. "Or maybe it's not the fame that made me unlikable. My parents didn't want to stay, which happened before I became a celebrity."

His words slice my heart in half. I'm bleeding out. It's the second time Cody has mentioned something about being liked. The first was the other day at brunch. I skipped over it because admitting that I *like* Cody, even as a friend, feels scary, as if that one admission will instantly lead my heart to more, but at the same time, I hate that he thinks it's his fault that everyone in his life has left him.

"You're not unlikable. You're just misunderstood."

The twitch of his mouth suggests a grin. "So how do I become *understood*?"

"By playing twenty questions, of course." I hope my

playful smirk lightens the conversation. Too much heaviness complicates my emotions.

"I'm starting to think you have stock in the twenty questions game. Do you get a penny every time someone asks a question?"

I keep my expression serious. "I don't have stock, but I am the official spokesperson."

The episode starts playing again, thankfully moving off from my ugly expression. Our eyes flip to the laptop, watching it for a second until a circle in the middle of the screen spins, stopping the movie on another equally horrifying mid-sentence face.

"Oh, come on!" I yell at the computer. "How come it doesn't ugly stop on you?"

"You don't look ugly." I shoot him a pointed stare, but he shrugs it off. "It's physically impossible for you not to look good." He grimaces as it skips to a new weird expression. "Except there." He points to the new face. "You look awful there."

I playfully kick him, but he dodges it by rolling off the bed to his feet.

"Wait here. I have portable Wi-Fi in my room that we can use to stream the show."

"Oh, now you say something? You could've mentioned your fancy Wi-Fi before the twenty minutes of buffering."

"And miss those *flattering* expressions from you? I don't think so." Cody throws me a smile as he opens the door. I throw a pillow, but it lands two feet in front of him just as he walks out.

CHAPTER
TWENTY

CODY

IT'S BEEN five excruciating days of filming, sometimes for sixteen hours straight, but we finally made it to filming the red dress scenes.

And although these moments take place in episode five, they're the last scenes we're filming since they involve the majority of the cast and the biggest set-up. We've saved the best for last, and I've been looking forward to filming it for a week now.

A lot of touching happens in these scenes.

And *the kiss*, which isn't just a measly kiss. It's a frenzied, hot makeout, and I'm more than ready to test Jenna's and my chemistry in that way. I have a feeling things will be very different from the first time we kissed in episode one.

Jenna and I have spent hours together on set every day. The uncomfortable awkwardness that was once between us has melted into friendship and maybe something more. Okay, it's more than friendship for me, but what, I don't know. I've never felt this way about a woman before. How do you define something you've never experienced? All I know is that I don't want it to end.

Teague and I stand in the middle of the ballroom, dressed in fitted suits. There's a gold crown on my head—a prop that's light enough that it's not too uncomfortable. We're waiting for everyone to be set and for Quinton to start rolling the cameras.

Teague stares at his phone, a small smile creeping over his lips.

"You must be texting your wife."

"She sent me a photo of her swollen ankles." He lifts his head and his phone, showing me the picture.

The old Cody wouldn't care and would probably be grossed out by a woman's pregnant ankles, but I find myself leaning in and laughing at the picture with Teague.

"Man, that sucks for her."

"Yeah, she says it's really itchy."

Another text from his wife follows the picture, the cliche, '*I love you. Miss you tons. Can't wait for you to come home tomorrow.*' My heart throbs as I read those simple words.

I've never wanted a serious relationship, marriage, or kids. I planned on being the eternal bachelor.

Forever.

So why am I all sad seeing a text like that from Teague's wife?

I guess in the back of my mind I'm wondering what it would feel like if someone sent me a text like that . . . and not just *someone*. What would it be like if Jenna said those words to me and actually meant them? Something tells me it would fill the bottomless hole inside me that I've been attempting to fill since I was a little kid.

That possibility makes my old plan of going nowhere with no one seem pointless. If given the choice between being alone the rest of my life or being with Jenna, I think I'd choose Jenna, and that's a startling revelation. Something nobody ever saw coming, especially me. I don't even know what to do with that revelation. It's a complete one-eighty turn from where I've been my entire life. How can something I've been so sure of—never wanting to get married or settle down—go up in flames in a matter of two weeks? I mean, that seems crazy. Or is there really something that special about Jenna?

"I just barely watched episode two last night. Have you seen it yet?" Teague asks, putting his phone in his pocket.

"Yeah, Jenna and I watched it last Friday when it came out."

"Together?" Teague's smile turns sly. "Are you sure that's all you did?"

I smack his chest with the back of my hand. "Yes, I'm sure."

Besides the wrestling for her computer, which I loved, we didn't touch at all. It was all very G-rated. Which is how it should be. I'm trying to be a good guy here. And then we've had another long week of no touching. Hence why I'm looking forward to filming today.

"What's the deal with you two? I know the relationship is all for show, but is something else going on?"

"No." I shake my head firmly. There's *nothing* else going on even though I'm starting to think I wouldn't be so opposed to it. "You know how these showmances go. It's just a publicity stunt."

"That's what I figured." Teague nods. "You and Jenna don't really work together, but it's definitely helping the show's ratings."

My gaze turns sour. "What do you mean we don't work together?"

Teague laughs. "Don't take offense. I'm just stating facts."

"I'm not offended." I try softening my voice so my words are somewhat believable. "I just don't know what you mean by that."

"Only that you two are different. Jenna is known for being sweet with high morals. She doesn't run around with guys like you."

"Actually, she's dated a lot of guys like me in the past." I don't know why I want Teague to know that. It's nothing for Jenna to brag about.

"And look where it's gotten her? Nowhere. I'm sure she's learned her lesson and is looking for someone serious she can settle down with. And that's definitely *not* you." Teague chuckles. "Am I right?"

"Yeah." I force a laugh, trying to replicate his. "You're totally right."

But after everything I just realized a moment ago, I hate Teague Morrow for being right about me.

"Alright, people!" Quinton uses a megaphone to reach all the cast and crew in the ballroom. "We're ready to film the iconic red dress scene." A few claps and cheers ripple through the crowd. "I want the reaction to be as real as possible. That's why we haven't brought Jenna in yet. Obviously, we'll do this in more than one take, but everyone stay in character, and let's make this take, when you're seeing her and the dress for the first time, our best one. Questions?" Nobody says anything. "Okay, places, please."

I tug on my lapel as Teague grabs a drink from the prop manager. Conversations fade. The crew clears out of the ballroom, and everything stills as the camera and sound start rolling. Naomi holds the sticks, calling out the scene number, and Quinton starts everything with a loud, "Action!"

Suddenly, the room buzzes with chatter and movement. The actors on the dais, playing prop instruments, start moving their arms back and forth, pretending to make music.

Teague turns to me and says something like he's my best friend, Drake. What we say right now doesn't matter. We just need to look like we're talking. He takes a long sip of his drink while I answer, but everything stops when Jenna takes her first step at the top of the giant staircase.

Teague does his part. He chokes on his drink just like planned.

But me, I don't even know what I'm supposed to do. My words trail to silence as I stare back at Jenna. I thought I was prepared for this part of the episode, thought I knew what to expect. I mean, it's just a dress. How impactful could it really be? But I'm stunned by her.

Jenna has never looked more beautiful. I dare someone to find me a time or a photoshoot that rivals this moment.

The strapless red dress rounds her body, enhancing it in the best ways. A lengthy slit shows every inch of her long legs, and each time she steps down the stairs, her legs get spotlighted.

I'm entranced by her descent.

I literally can't look away.

I've been in show business a long time. I've worked side by side with some of the most stunning women in all of Hollywood. They've worn dresses made specifically for their bodies, had their hair and makeup professionally done.

But nothing compares to Jenna.

My heart races as I watch her deliver her lines to each key character that approaches as she slowly makes her way through the ballroom. I'm cognizant of the cameras moving around us and how one rotates in front of me and Teague in preparation for our part.

"It's the dress from the magazine," Teague says with admiration, acting like Drake.

"I . . ." I think my line starts with that, but I've been so unfocused I can't really be sure, and now Jenna is headed toward us, and it's getting harder to remember.

She!

That's my next line.

"She . . . looks way better than the magazine. How did she . . ."

Jenna stops in front of us, and I can't help but smile at her as I gawk.

"Good evening, gentlemen." She dips into a curtsy, and

my eyes follow, checking her out the entire time, but they're supposed to for the sake of the show—that much I remember. So I keep looking, not even trying to hide my wandering gaze.

When she comes up, the smugness on her face is genuine. She's not Renna Degray. She's Jenna Lewis, and she knows exactly what she's doing to me.

JENNA IS the first person I find when we wrap up filming for the dance scene. I just spent the last two hours holding her in my arms, pulling her body as close to mine as the script allowed, but it wasn't enough. I want more, an insatiable desire that never feels satisfied.

She's alone, off to the side of the set, back pressed against the wall.

I drop my gaze over her body, still blown away by her in that red dress. Her eyes lift as I approach, and immediately, sparks ignite, fueling my body with heat.

My hand goes to my chest as if it can somehow contain my hammering heart.

Her eyebrows pull upward, waiting for me to say something.

"You're killing me today," I finally say.

"Just today?" Her flirty smile turns my world upside down.

"No, not *just* today. But definitely right now. That red dress is doing its job. I'm a mess."

"I know. You kept forgetting your lines."

"Was I that obvious?"

"A little."

"Well, I was more than a little enamored with you."

Still am.

Jenna's blush and smile combine together, adding to her charm. "At least Quinton is happy about it. We're finally giving him chemistry."

I walk around her body, leaning my shoulder against the wall next to where she stands. Her head follows my movement, two sultry green eyes staring back at me.

I understand what Quinton meant when he said he wanted us to have so much chemistry he could build a state-of-the-art chemistry lab. At this point, we could build ten chemistry labs with everything brewing between us.

"It's good we hit our stride in time for these moments. It may be our last day of filming, but I think we got the hang of it now." My foot shuffles closer in an attempt to ease the longing gripping my chest. I don't even know what I'm longing for. Her body. Her mind. Her soul. I think I want it all.

"It's good since we film the kiss next." She turns her body toward me, leaning her shoulder against the wall as well.

I feel like I'm in the middle of a *Mother, May I?* game.

Mother, may I take one giant step toward Jenna?

Yes, you may.

I forge ahead another inch or two. "The infamous kiss."

"Do you think it will go better this time around?"

"Is this your way of asking if I ate a garlic tuna fish sandwich at lunch?"

She laughs, gently letting her head fall back, and it's all I can do not to dive forward and trail my lips down her neck.

"Did you eat a garlic tuna fish sandwich at lunch?"

I shake my head. "Not today."

"That's really good news for me."

"And what about you?" My eyes fall over her bare shoulder and arm. "Are you experiencing any hives over kissing me?"

"Not today." She takes a small step to me. "Although, who knows? We never did practice the kiss in Malibu."

Practice? Heck, if she'd let me, I'd clear everything off the table across from us and practice the kiss right here and now. I'm confident it could hold the weight of both our bodies.

"Maybe we don't need practice." Another step forward, but this time, the toe of my shoe bumps into hers. "Maybe we just need to feel what our characters feel. Immerse ourselves in their emotions."

"Like method acting?" She leans closer since there's no more room to gain with our feet.

"Yeah." I meet her halfway with a lean of my own. "You know, embody our roles with complete emotional assimilation."

"So, you're Trev." She smiles. "And I'm Renna."

"That's right."

"And we're in love but can't be together."

"But we want to."

"We *definitely* want to." Her words are throaty, causing my chest to go wild.

If I narrowed the space between us any more, it would put our lips touching—a very tempting prospect. So tempting that my eyes drop to her mouth, contemplating it without planning to act on it. I can wait a few more minutes.

I force my gaze back to her eyes. "So what do you say? Are you willing to throw everything into our characters? No holding back?"

"No holding back." Her eyes drop to my lips too—an undetectable movement so quick I almost missed it. But it was there.

"For the sake of the show," I say.

"For the sake of the show."

"We're ready for you both," Naomi calls from across the room.

Neither one of us pulls back or looks away.

I think we're ready for this too.

CHAPTER TWENTY-ONE

JENNA

I THOUGHT we were filming the kiss scene.

In my mind, that meant our lips would be locked and loaded within two minutes of, '*Roll camera!*'

Not the case.

We've been at it for an hour, filming every last detail that leads up to the kiss, but not the *actual* kiss.

Don't get me wrong. That's all important stuff, and it involved touching. Lots of delicious touching between Cody and me. His hands were on my bare shoulders and arms. His fingers brushed against mine, intertwining with tenderness that was achingly sweet. But all of that just makes me want the kiss even more.

It's been one hour of foreplay, and if you combine that with the ballroom scenes we filmed all morning, it's more like eight hours of excruciating build-up. I don't think I've ever anticipated something so much, and yes, I once was a kid on Christmas Eve, waiting for my Felicity American Girl doll. That moment doesn't even compare to this.

But there's nothing else left to film.

It's time, and by the charged glances Cody and I keep exchanging, we're both more than ready.

"I don't want to choreograph every last detail of this scene," Quinton says, looking between us. "I want each touch to feel organic, to build naturally. So stay in character as long as you need. We'll keep the cameras rolling, especially if you guys are feeling it."

Oh, I'm feeling it.

Wanting it.

I've been suppressing my attraction to Cody for so long, telling myself I can't give in. But today, I'm *supposed* to give in. I'm supposed to channel everything Renna feels for Trev and deliver a kiss that has audiences searching it up on YouTube for years to come.

It's all the permission I need.

"Okay, let's take it from where we left off," Quinton directs. "Jenna, your back is against the curtains with one hand on Cody's chest."

Cody slips in front of me, and I slowly lift my hand, placing it over his heart. The intensity of his beats matches what's happening in my chest, and we haven't even begun filming.

"No holding back?" he whispers as the cameras start rolling. His blazing eyes hold so much passion I wouldn't be surprised if he were one of those cartoon characters that shoots laser beams every time he looks at something.

"No holding back," I say as Quinton yells, "Action!"

I'm all in.

Feeling *everything* my character would feel.

I watch in anticipation as Cody's eyes drop to my lips, then slowly lift, meeting my stare with an intensity I can't even comprehend. I'm fixed against the wall, waiting for him to make the first move. Our gazes hold steady as he lowers his head to mine. At the last second, I close my eyes, concentrating on the soft skims of his lips and the brush of his beard against my skin. Everything is slow and restrained, even how his hands hold my waist. I feel valuable in his arms, like an antique he plans to delicately take care of for the rest of his life.

The kiss is all about our lips, how they snag and catch with every lightly flirtatious and playfully seductive graze. We're feeling each other's energy, trusting and believing that, *together*, we know what the moment needs.

And we both know we need *more*.

Cody pulls back just enough to scan my eyes. We share a fleeting moment, a charged stare before agonizing desire drives us forward again. Our bodies collide with all the force of repressed passion, with every ounce of chemistry we've built but never acted on.

The kiss becomes a dynamic dance, a tango of physicality with raw passion, sensuality, and strong emotions. I once thought Cody and I had nothing in common, but our physical closeness tells a different story. It's a window to an intimate connection bigger than anything I've ever experienced.

In Malibu, he asked how I liked to be held, but he already seems to know. His hands press against my back, pushing my body closer, and I willingly come, loving the feeling of being wanted, desired in a way that he's helpless against.

I comb my fingers through the back of his hair—something I've dreamed about a hundred times. I hold his body to me, feeling every hard line of his chest and arms—another thing I've dreamed about a hundred times. And I return his fevered kiss with my own desperate need for gratification.

I focus on Cody's taste, smell, arms, his hold against my body, and the heaviness of his chest pressed against mine. It all triggers an intensity inside me, a g-force I can't withstand. The kiss heightens, changes, spins to new levels as our bodies learn and grow together. We're weightless, falling through time in a beyond-vertical drop filled with ecstasy and thrill.

Each second that ticks on, we obliterate the unspoken rules and lines.

Feelings are no longer suppressed.

There are no more restrictions.

No holding back.

"Queen Marielle said her line."

I don't stop.

"You're supposed to break apart. Queen Marielle said her line."

Cody doesn't stop.

"Cody! Jenna!"

That's enough to yank us out of our blissful fantasy, lurching us into stark reality.

We're filming. *Film-ing.*

This is a place of work. A job. A set.

There's a cast. A crew. A slew of watching people.

We're characters in a show. Trev. Renna. *The Promised Prince.*

All that information comes tumbling to the front of my mind in horrifying awareness as my eyes sweep around the room. With each new realization, I slowly unpeel myself from Cody.

Whispers ripple through the room as pairs of eyes gawk at us. Everyone knows that a lot more than acting just happened with that kiss.

My stare stops on Quinton, and my face heats with indescribable embarrassment as I assess his expression. "We've been trying to get your attention for a minute now. Queen Marielle even said her line. You two were supposed to break apart."

"We didn't…" Cody's voice is hoarse. He clears his throat as he shakes his head. "*I* didn't hear it."

Quinton's gaze flips between us like a principal trying to decide who to blame for the food fight in the lunchroom. There's a subtle nod. Then his eyes swing around the room to the crew. "Let's take thirty minutes to give our actors a break, and then we'll reset."

To give our actors a break?

What he means is, let's give Cody and Jenna a second to cool off so this very fake and fictional kiss no longer turns them on.

More whispers travel through the room.

I prefer the hives over this level of emotional humiliation.

Cody's piercing stare follows me as I walk out of the room.

CODY

WHEN YOU'RE AN ACTOR, nobody thinks twice when you live your life in fiction, when you *become* your character. In fact, they shower you with compliments. Congratulate you on immersing yourself in your role. Admire you for being so committed to your craft. Heck, they even give you awards for staying so true with your portrayal.

Well, where's my freaking Academy Award?

Because what just happened in there was the complete and total embodiment of my character—that's the lie I'm going to tell myself because the truth is too damning.

We did the kiss scene in *one take*.

Do you know how rare the one-take wonder is? It's rare.

Quinton kept the cameras rolling when Jenna and I finally broke apart. I guess our shocked and dazed expressions were good enough to use in the episode. All we had to do was pick up our lines from after the kiss and finish the dialogue.

I'm not sure if I should be relieved that we didn't have to kiss again or completely depressed.

"Hey, you okay?" Teague pops his head into my trailer after filming.

I look up from my spot at the dining table. "One take."

He shoots me a sly smile. "Were you hoping for more chances to kiss Jenna?"

"I think I kissed her plenty good the first time."

"You really got into it, didn't you?"

"Was it that obvious?"

"Uh, yeah." He coughs out a laugh.

I swipe my hand down my face, trying to wipe the memory out of my mind. Not specifically the kiss memory, just the memory of losing myself during filming and everyone knowing it.

"Relax. It's not that big of a deal." Teague steps inside, letting the door shut behind him. "A lot of actors get lost in on-screen kisses. That's why there are intimacy coaches. You're trying to make it look real, so real feelings are going to get involved. It happens all the time."

But not to me.

I press my clenched fist against my mouth, not sure what to say.

He takes my silence as permission to keep his speech going. "It's the sign of a good method actor when you take your character's feelings and make them your own."

"I know what method acting is."

The problem is, I wasn't method acting.

I wasn't *acting* at all when I kissed Jenna.

I wasn't thinking about Trev, the story, or what the scene called for. I was only thinking about what I *wanted*. Because if I were thinking about her or the movie, I wouldn't have behaved that way. I wouldn't have lost myself in the kiss or how good it felt to hold her in my arms. From the moment our lips touched, all reason and logic were abandoned, replaced by strong emotional and physical desires.

"So you're a good method actor, right alongside Daniel Day-Lewis or Leo DiCaprio. It's fine. That's when the magic happens."

Oh, magic definitely happened, just not in the way Teague thinks.

"Nobody in his right mind would blame you for letting things get a little too heated with Jenna. She's considered one of the sexiest women in the world. It would take a blind man to keep lust and carnal desires in check while working with her. So don't sweat it. It's part of the job."

Falling for my costar is part of the job?

"Maybe even a perk of the job." He elbows me with a smirk. "But we're done filming the show. We'll fly home tomorrow, and after the wrap party, you don't have to see Jenna again." Except, tomorrow, I'm her date for her brother's wedding, but Teague doesn't need to know the details of my schedule. "And if Flixmart picks up season two, you'll only be in a few scenes together. No big deal."

I lift my brows, placating him. "You're right."

"On to the next project, my friend." He slaps me on the back. "I'll see you in LA at the wrap party." He gives me a half-wave before exiting my trailer.

I don't say goodbye because I'm still stuck on his *lust and carnal desires* comment from earlier. Teague makes me sound like a typical playboy, just in it for instant gratification.

Okay, yes. There was some lust. And a heck of a lot of desire. But—BUT—there was so much more to the kiss than that. There was a deepness I wasn't anticipating (probably because it was supposed to be an on-screen kiss, not a real one). I felt connected to Jenna emotionally. I wanted her to feel cherished and special and beautiful. And in return, I wanted her acceptance and reassurance that despite everything in my past, I'm worthy of her respect and love.

What in the world am I even saying? I've turned into that guy. The guy I hate that says words like *cherished* and actually feels things.

I don't do feelings.

My testosterone levels must be at an all-time low. At any

minute, I could start crying over kittens, or lactating, or something else completely unlike me.

This has to stop.

I don't even recognize myself anymore or the change happening inside my head and heart.

I drop to the ground, throwing out one hundred pushups —the manliest thing I can come up with on the spot. I also yell out a string of profanities while doing my pushups, just for an added macho effect.

What the heck is Jenna Lewis doing to me?

CHAPTER
TWENTY-TWO

JENNA

NEITHER CODY nor I mentioned the kiss last night as we wrapped up filming *The Promised Prince*. We didn't talk about it early this morning when we took a car to the airport, boarded the Flixmart jet, or during our six-hour flight from Calgary to Tampa to attend my brother's wedding.

We didn't avoid each other. We just moved on as if the whole thing didn't happen.

And maybe it didn't. Maybe for Cody, this is typical movie stuff. You share a mind-blowing kiss with your costar and then go home to your girlfriend. Except, today, I'm Cody's girlfriend.

We fake being in love for the show. And we fake being in love for real life.

We're like the movie *Inception*—two levels deep, a dream within a dream. And I'm starting to lose my grip on reality. I need a spinning top to help me differentiate between it all. I mean, it worked for Leo in the movie, so why not me?

In addition to losing my grip on reality, the walls around my heart are crumbling, and with my defenses down, I'm vulnerable to all of Cody's charms.

Allll of them.

Namely his kiss.

And the confident way he held me in his arms as if he had no doubt in his mind that he'd deliver the best kiss of my life. And it was. It was *the best* kiss of my life—the difference maker.

Now I'm left wanting more.

I tossed and turned all night, replaying our kiss from different angles as if I were the director, focusing on every touch, caress, and brush of our lips—the controlled and the frenzied.

At midnight, I cranked up the AC.

At two a.m., I drank an entire glass of water.

At three a.m., I splashed cold water on my face.

And by six a.m., when my alarm went off, I took an ice-cold shower to try and cool down my overheated body.

I earned these puffy bags under my eyes. But they're nothing a little bit of concealer can't hide.

Luckily, Cody and I slept on the plane ride from Calgary to Tampa. We arrived at Trey's yacht an hour and a half ago. Winnie had a hair and makeup artist waiting for me on the dock. They whisked me to my room while Cody showered in one of the other guest bedrooms.

But now everything is quiet. I stare at myself in the mirror. I'm wearing a teal two-piece dress. The top is a spaghetti strap, fitted crop, and the bottom is a high-waisted skirt with a deep slit over the right leg. I'm a bridesmaid for the wedding but not in the traditional sense. I picked out my own dress, and I don't have to walk down the aisle or stand in a line next to Whitney. Since this is her second wedding, she just wants it to be her and Trey at the bow of the boat as they say their vows.

Two knocks rap on the door, and I turn. "Come in."

"There she is." Trey peeks his head around the door with a smile as giant as his frame.

I shake my head, looking him over as he steps inside. "You look so handsome."

"You think?" His hands brush down the front of his three-piece black tuxedo. "I'm sweating a lot. Not because I'm nervous. Just excited."

"You should be excited. This is a big day and a long time coming."

He nods a few times, looking at me with a big-brother protectiveness I've always admired about him. "Thanks for being here."

"You act as if I wouldn't come."

"I just know how busy you are, and I really appreciate you taking the time out of your—"

"Stop!" I groan. "I would never miss this day."

"It looks like your fake boyfriend wouldn't miss it either." Trey's smile teases.

"I'm the worst!" My eyes widen. "I forgot to tell you I was bringing Cody. I mean, Tawny made me, but I still should've warned you."

"It's fine. At least now I get to see your acting skills live. Not just on the big screen."

"Oh, yeah, my acting skills." I laugh, but it doesn't sound too convincing.

"The relationship is still fake, right?"

"Yes." I scratch the back of my neck. "I mean, I think so."

"What does that mean?"

"Well, we kissed."

"Really?" His eyebrows jump to his hairline.

"In the episode, not in real life, but it didn't feel like an on-screen kiss. It felt real, so now I don't know what's happening."

"What do you want to happen?"

"I don't know."

"Three weeks ago, when this fake relationship started, you

didn't want to fall for Cody because you thought he'd just break your heart like every other guy."

"He might." I bite my lip, looking back at Trey. "But he might not. I'm starting to wonder if I've been wrong about him this whole time. He might actually be different than the others."

"The only way to know for sure is to put your heart out there and see what happens."

"How can I do that when I don't even know what's real between us and what's fake?"

"Ask him." Trey shrugs.

That seems scary. It's mature, adult behavior but scary nonetheless.

"If what's happening between you is real, give Cody a shot to be the man you want. If it's fake, well…" Trey shrugs as his words dangle, neither of us needing him to finish his thought. We both know I'd be brokenhearted once again.

"You know, it's not fair that you have to give me advice on your wedding day. I'm the one that should be leaving you with words of wisdom to ponder."

"Oh, don't worry. Dad already did that."

"He did?" My nose scrunches.

"Yeah, he said, 'Trey, I think you're making a mistake by marrying that woman. There's still time to back out.'"

"No!" I pull my brother into a hug. "Why is he such a jerk to you?"

"It's fine." Trey's laughter rumbles against my body. "There's nothing Dad could say that would make me change my mind about Whitney. His opinion or anyone else's doesn't matter. I know who she is and why she took the road she took. I love her, and I know she loves me. Nothing else matters."

His words hit me hard, not because of him and Whitney, but because of Cody. I've spent the last five months convincing myself that he wasn't a good guy, that he's a serial dater, that he plays games, and that he will absolutely break my heart if I give him the chance. The story I keep telling myself about him is largely based on other people's opinions and on what I've seen and read about him over the years. But I'm slowly learning he's not that guy. Maybe all the other noise doesn't matter if I know who Cody is. What I think about him and *us* is the only opinion that counts.

TWENTY-THREE

CODY

SUNRAYS DANCE across the water as Trey's million-dollar yacht pulls out of the harbor. Music from the live string quartet perched on the upper deck floats down to the A-list wedding guests. Most of them are athletes and recognizable sportscasters from television, making me the only Hollywood star here besides Jenna.

And I'm not saying that as a flex or a brag. I'm saying that because I have no one to talk to. Literally, I'm leaning against the side of the boat, sipping champagne *alone* while Jenna gets ready. But I'm not really alone. Everyone knows who I am, and their eyes keep drifting to me. Not to mention the speed boats trailing alongside us, holding paparazzi trying to catch a glimpse of the guests. I'm at this wedding because of them and their long lenses.

"Cody, it's good to see you again," a deep voice says behind me.

My body turns, and in front of me stands Larry Lewis, Jenna's dad, and her mother, Marlena. I briefly met them at the premier a few weeks ago.

I shift my drink from one hand to the other so I can shake his. "Same to you."

Marlena beams at me, taking my hands and hugging them to her chest. "I'm so glad you could join us this evening." She's a lot like Jenna, beautiful in that timeless way with a tall, thin frame and blonde hair, although her mother's is cut short to her chin.

"I am too." I smile back at them. "Congratulations on such a wonderful day."

I've never congratulated anyone on getting married or for their son getting married. I know that's the typical sentiment at weddings, but I never do it. Nothing about the institution of marriage seems like something we should celebrate. That would be like saying, 'I'm so happy and excited for you that in five to twenty years, you'll realize this relationship is doomed, hurt and destroy the one person you said you loved, and try to get out of the marriage without looking like it's your fault that it fell apart.' But I spare Jenna's parents my true feelings and stick to the scripted well wishes.

"I have to say"—Larry lifts his chin, upping his intimidation game—"I'm surprised you're here with Jenna. All I've ever heard is how much she dislikes working with you."

"Larry!" Marlena's tone is embarrassed. "Just ignore him."

"What? I can't call out another man's intentions when it comes to my daughter?"

"It's fine. I'd do the same thing if I were a father. But I think Jenna's incredible. She's smart, talented, funny, kind, and when I'm with her, I want to be a better man."

The relationship we're faking might not be true, but everything I think and feel about her is.

"Awww." Marlena places her hand over her heart. "See, Larry? There's nothing to worry about. Cody is a pure gentleman."

He scoffs. "I'm not as gullible as my wife. But then again, I didn't marry her for her brains." Larry waves his wife away with the flick of a few fingers. "Marlena, why don't you run along and check on the decorations while the men have a real conversation? Man to man."

My gaze flicks to Jenna's mom, watching how her eyes dim despite the perfectly controlled smile on her face. "I'm sure there's some kind of last-minute wedding thing that needs to be attended to." She forces her smile wider. "It was lovely talking to you."

Talking to me? Her jack-a-husband didn't even give her the chance to talk.

"Mrs. Lewis?" My hand lightly touches her forearm before she walks away. "Anyone who can't appreciate what a classy, intelligent woman you are is a disappointment. I'd love to talk to you later. Maybe you'd even do me the honor of a dance?"

Her smile turns soft and appreciative. "I'd really like that." Before walking away, her eyes melt into a glare. She aims it at her husband, then leaves.

"You think I don't know what you're doing here?" Larry's stony gaze falls on me. "For once in your life, you're trying to come off as the good guy, and you're using my family to do it. First with Jenna, and now with my wife. I've seen the headlines about how you use women. Jenna might be too stupid and naive to recognize it, but I'm not. So I suggest you move along and find a new toy to play with."

I laugh in an irritated way that doesn't hold any semblance of humor. "I feel bad for you. You have your trophy wife, your NFL son, and your supermodel daughter, and you actually think that everyone's success and achievements are because of you when, really, it's all *in spite of* you." I take a step forward, lowering my voice. "You obviously don't know your daughter, because if you did, you'd know there's nothing stupid or naive about her." I look down at him with a puff of a mocking laugh. "I'd take a good long look in the mirror because I'm not the one that uses or doesn't appreciate the women in my life."

With that, I turn and walk away, heading to the other end of the boat. My blood boils with anger. It all makes sense. Jenna's terrible choices in men funnel back to her dad, and she doesn't even see it. She's just repeating the same pattern of behavior that her mom fell into, choosing men who only want a beautiful woman by their side, not a companion.

I lean against the side of the yacht, glancing behind my shoulder, hoping Jenna will be coming out soon. I feel like she's been getting ready for hours. She's nowhere to be found, but my eyes catch a familiar face from my Google search of Jenna's dating history. It's the sports agent, the one who became a meme for being jealous of another woman while he was dating Jenna. He's here with the woman, and she's pregnant—must be his now wife.

Great. Another prick in Jenna's life to deal with.

His gaze locks with mine, and he smiles. *Smiles.* He clearly can't read my mind.

Oh, now he's coming over.

"Cody, right?" His arm extends, so I shake his hand. What else am I going to do? Punch him? "You're here with Jenna?"

"Yeah." My jaw hardens as our hands break apart. This guy has chosen the worst time to come and talk to me. Larry Lewis has already primed me with anger.

"I'm Ben Jackson, a friend of both Trey and Jenna."

"I know who you are. You're the jerk who was in love with his best friend while you were dating Jenna. Real cool to play with her heart like that." My words come out harsh, and instead of being offended, this guy's lips lift as if he's amused.

"What I did to Jenna wasn't cool." At least he can admit it. "But I'd like to think I wasn't that big of a jerk. I mean, Trey and Jenna still like me despite everything, so I couldn't have been that bad."

"Well," I scoff, "Jenna is the nicest person I've ever met

and likes almost everyone." *Everyone except for me.* "So we can't really base anything off of that." I take a sip of my drink, glancing away from him.

"She is the nicest person. I'm glad to see you think so too. And what about you?" His question prompts me to look back at him. "Are you playing with Jenna's heart?"

Is this guy serious? Is he really asking me about *my* intentions with Jenna?

I take a step forward, standing right in front of Ben. We're about the same height and build, so it's not like I have some intimidation factor giving me the edge here, but the step makes me feel better nonetheless. "You don't have to worry about me. I'm not playing a game with Jenna's heart. I know what I am, and I know what she deserves."

Ben's mouth drifts into a wide smile. Why is he smiling so much? It's creepy.

"Good." He nods a few times. "I better get back to my wife, but it was nice to meet you."

I glare at him as he walks away. Jenna thinks I'm bad. Dude, that guy is a classic player—but he's married, so I guess he's not. But I still don't like him or the fool he made out of her.

"Psst!"

My brows lower as I look around.

"Psst! Over here."

I spin, following the sound to an old lady sitting in a wheelchair by the couch.

"Are you talking to me?" I point to my chest. I think I liked this wedding better when I was alone and had no one to talk to. People are coming out of the woodwork to chat now. I feel like I'm being punked.

"No, I'm talking to the fish in the ocean," the old woman snaps. "Of course, I'm talking to you!"

I walk to her. "Do you need something?"

Her wrinkled finger wags in front of my face. "You should go shirtless more often in your movies. Women like that."

My brows jump in surprise, and a small laugh billows out. "Uh, thank you. I think."

"I bet Jenna likes your abs. I would."

"Um." I glance around, looking for the hidden cameras. I'm definitely being punked. "I'm sorry. Who are you?"

"Gia Savittieri." She holds her hand out, floppy like a dead fish. "The bride's grandma."

"It's nice to meet you, Gia." I clasp my fingers over her hand. It's not a real shake, more like an awkward hold. "Cody Banner."

"Pfft." Her lips vibrate together. "You think I don't know who you are? You're the sexiest man alive. I know who you are."

"That's just a title. I'm not sure how much truth there is to it."

Her beady eyes travel up and down my body. "There's plenty of truth to it. You're with Jenna, the supermodel?"

"Uh, yeah. I'm her date today."

"Do you love her?"

"Oh, boy." I rub the edges of my beard. "We're just figuring things out still."

That beady stare gets more intense, as if she's trying to look into my soul. "You love her."

I surprise laugh. Who is this lady?

"Gia!" Jenna comes from nowhere, bending down to hug the grandma in her wheelchair.

She's wearing a fitted teal dress, and when she leans in to hug, I make the mistake of appraising her backside, which looks fantastic, but that's beside the point. Because the second my eyes drop to her body, this little Italian grandma smirks and winks. She watched me check out Jenna's butt and apparently approves.

Weirdest wedding of my life.

I don't even know what's happening right now or how I feel about it.

"How are you doing?" Jenna asks the old lady as she straightens.

"Enough about me." She grabs Jenna's hand and puts it in mine. "There. He's been waiting for you."

Jenna's green eyes peek at me as her lips twitch. "He's going to have to wait a little bit longer because the ceremony is about to start." She pulls her hand out of my grasp and stands behind the wheelchair. "Let me take you to your spot." As she starts to walk away, she turns over her shoulder, throwing me the best smile I've ever seen. "Don't go anywhere."

I wouldn't go anywhere even if I knew I was standing on a nuclear target when the missile has just been launched.

I'm here for her.

JENNA

SOFT MUSIC PLAYS as Whitney walks down the aisle toward Trey. I can't help the tears in my eyes as I watch the expression on both of their faces. Complete happiness. That's the only way to describe it. And that's the number one thing I hope to find someday. The preacher tells everyone to be seated, and I slowly drop into my chair.

Cody's arm immediately wraps around my shoulder, pulling me close to him like he did in the interview. I relax into his hard chest and feel the warmth of his body press against my skin.

Everything has been so crazy since we got here that I haven't even had a chance to talk to him. I barely even saw him before the ceremony, but I let my eyes wander to him now.

My stomach spins at the sight of him in his tuxedo. The color matches the blackness of his dark hair that curls at the base of his neck. He has on his signature sunglasses, looking sexier than any man should ever look, and when he shifts his head toward me, my breath stalls from the complete picture of his handsomeness.

He leans in. "I didn't have a chance to tell you, but you look stunning. I don't want to take my eyes off you." Soft whispers dance across my neck, combining with his sultry tone —a tone that can only be described as a bedroom voice. I shudder, feeling each goosebump trail down my skin. I wish I could see the heated look I know is behind his sunglasses.

I turn my head forward, but just as I do, Cody's free hand rests on my upper thigh. I glance down to where my slit opens over my crossed legs. His thumb draws circles on my bare skin. It's amazing, and explosive, and the most distracting thing I've ever experienced.

Paparazzi circle us in speed boats, but none of them would be able to see Cody's hand on my thigh. None of them would be able to catch in a photograph the protective way he holds me. But I don't care.

I want Cody to touch me this way, even if nobody sees it.

CHAPTER
TWENTY-FOUR

JENNA

THE SUN HAS LONG SET, and so has the quiet reverence of the ceremony. Music with a beat thumps, vibrating the entire boat. Ties, jackets, and shoes have all been removed and discarded to the side as the after-party picks up steam.

Cody and I dance under stringed lights in the middle of the floor, surrounded by Trey, Whitney, and the very rambunctious Tampa Bay offensive line—these men know how to party. Damien Wallace—I think he's the running back—has moves that put Michael Jackson to shame.

One fast song ends, transitioning into another. But I need a break and some air. I thought I did a lot of cardio, but one hour of straight dancing and jumping has done me in.

I lean into Cody, shouting above the music. "I'm going to go get a drink. Do you want something?"

"I'll come with you." He grabs my hand, leading me through the crowd to the back of the boat. "What do you want?"

"Water." I fan myself, signaling that I'm overheated in addition to being dehydrated.

"I'll get you some." He lets go and walks to where the bar is. I watch for a second as he leans against the counter, trying to get the bartender's attention. His rolled-up sleeves and unbuttoned white shirt that shows glimpses of his chest are going to be my undoing.

"Jenna!"

I spin to see Ben Jackson and his wife, Brooke, behind me. "I haven't seen you all night," he says, pulling me into a hug.

"I know! I'm sorry. I arrived right before the ceremony, and then it's been so crazy." I glance down at Brooke's baby bump. "I was thrilled when Trey told me the news." I really was, but there was also a wave of longing, an *I-wish-that-were-me-having-a-baby* moment. But I push those thoughts aside and smile back at her. "When are you due?"

"Three months."

"It's a boy." Ben pats her stomach. "And you better believe that as soon as he can walk, I'm bringing him over to Trey to learn how to catch a football."

"Ben, I don't think that's going to work." Brooke looks at him. "He'll have your genes, and you're not half as coordinated as Trey."

"Oh, come on!" Ben whines.

I smile, watching the two of them together.

Brooke turns to me. "I'm going to sit down inside, but we just wanted to say hi before the night was over."

"I'm so glad you did."

"And"—Ben glances to where Cody is standing at the bar —"I wanted to tell you I met Cody Banner."

"Yeah, we're costars in that Flixmart series I'm doing."

At this point, we might be more than costars, but I'm not about to explain the complexity of our relationship to Ben and Brooke.

"We've watched every episode of *The Promised Prince* that has aired," Ben says.

"Even the one that came out today." Brooke laughs. "Ben

is obsessed. We had to get it in before we could get ready for the wedding this afternoon."

"I'm not obsessed. I just need to know what happens next. But anyway"—he shakes his head as if he doesn't know how we got so far off track from the conversation he wants to have —"I talked to Cody, and I just wanted you to know that the guy is absolutely in love with you."

"What?" The word comes out as a breathy laugh. "Why do you think that? What did he say?" My questions are fast and urgent.

"I don't remember exactly what he said."

"Ben, you need to do better than that. We want word for word," Brooke explains. "You can't tell Jenna that Cody loves her and then not remember what he said that made you think that."

"Yes, word for word would be appreciated."

"Well, he was possessive, jealous, and hates me, which we all know is a sign of being in love."

"But what did he say?" I press.

After some thought, his face lights with recollection. "I think he said, 'I'm not playing a game with Jenna's heart. I know what I am, and I know what she deserves.' Yeah, that's it. That's what he said." He smiles like he's proud of himself.

My eyes drift to Cody as his words settle. He's noticed me talking to Ben. His expression has hardened, and his back is straight as he stretches his neck to see us better.

"See?" Ben points over to him. "See the jealousy? He's about to come fight me to defend your honor. He's totally in love with you but doesn't know it yet, so be gentle with him. A guy like Cody Banner will be in denial for a while, convincing himself he's better off alone."

Brooke smiles up at him. "Sounds like someone else I know."

"Yeah, it does." He shrugs, knowing she's talking about

him. "Anyway, I better get Brooke inside so she can sit down. Good luck with Cody."

Ben and Brooke walk away, leaving me standing there with all my shock.

And hope.

Freak! I have hope.

That's the number one thing I shouldn't have. But despite my best efforts at acting, I've muddied the waters. I've fallen for Cody Banner. And I'm starting to wonder—like, *really* wonder—if he's feeling the same way.

Cody fights his way through the guests, walking to me with two glasses of ice water. "What did that Ben guy want?" His voice is hard, and yes, I can see the jealousy in his expression. It's cute.

My lips tilt into a smile. "Are you jealous?"

"Of that guy? What? No!" He hands me my water. "Ben Jackson is a jerk, and you deserve better."

I smother my smile so I can actually take a drink of my water without spilling it down my chest. Cody walks to the edge of the yacht, casting his eyes over the moonlit water and Tampa City's twinkling lights in the distance. I follow, pressing my hips against the railing.

"It's nice to be somewhere else for a change," he says. "I like making movies and filming, but every once in a while, you need a break."

"It's too bad that on your first day off, you have to spend it with me and my family."

Cody turns his head, giving me a smile that's so dang sweet it sends my body into diabetic shock. "There's nowhere else I'd rather be."

I want to believe him. I want to enjoy the skip in my heart and the butterflies in my stomach. I want what he's saying to be real. I want it so bad that I don't even stop myself when my next words slip out.

"Is that real, or is that fake?"

Cody's smile widens, reaching his eyes and making him look so handsome it hurts. He shifts his body so his hip leans against the side of the boat, and he faces me. "What do you think?"

"I don't know what to think anymore. I don't know what's real and what's acting."

"Then ask me."

I narrow my eyes. "I thought I just did."

"You're right." He rests his elbow on the railing, putting his hand next to my arm. His fingers tickle back and forth along my skin, and his eyes glimmer. "I've loved spending the day with you: real. I think you're the most beautiful woman I've ever seen: real."

His fingers slowly trickle up my arm, over my shoulder, across the edge of my collarbone, and into my hair. He combs his fingers through a few strands, pushing them back until he can tuck them behind my ear. Don't mind me. I'm just heavy breathing over here while his touch does all the work.

"I think you're the most talented and incredible woman I've ever known: real. You make me want to be a better man: real. I want you to be happy: real."

And the kiss?

Was that real?

Please tell me that was real.

But instead, he goes in a different direction.

"I Googled your dating history: real."

A flattered smile stretches across my mouth. "You Googled me?"

"I had to know what I'm up against." His fingers drift down my arm, stopping at my hand, staying there.

"No one worth mentioning." I glance away, embarrassed by my past heartbreaks and what Google says about them.

His eyes fill with tenderness. "You deserve better than what you've had: real. You deserve someone who's going to love and adore you: real. You deserve a man who appreciates you for all the right reasons, who's committed and will treat you well: real."

There's that hope again, funneling into my heart like a strategy worth pinning my entire life's happiness on.

I want Cody to be that guy. I want him to love me so much that all his doubts and fears about love and marriage go away. I don't want to be with him for ratings or magazine stories. I want to be with him because it's right.

I look straight into his eyes. "Do you know where I can find a man like that? Because I'm tired of looking for him."

His fingers lace through mine, and he lifts our hands, hanging them in the air between us. "Maybe you've been looking in the wrong places."

"I *know* I've been looking in the wrong places."

"Maybe I can help with your search." His other hand slips around my hip. I feel his fingers slide over the skin at my waist —the slowest, most sensual touch of my life. His lips kick up in his flirty way. "He'd have to be handsome."

"Definitely." I smile as he pulls my body to his.

"And charming."

I wrap my arms around his neck. "That's a given."

"A great sense of style." His lips press softly against my cheek and neck. "Popular among the ladies, but not a ladies' man. The most exquisite chest, arms, and six-pack you've ever seen. An arrogant, bad-boy persona that you find wildly attractive. And a good kisser." He pulls back with a playful smile. "Your words. Not mine."

"How often do you have to read my accidental text to be able to recite it off the cuff like that?"

"I read that text every night: real."

His words draw out my laugh. "Well, sounds like you've described the perfect guy." My expression turns serious. "But he's only perfect if he feels the same way I do."

"And if he did?" Cody smiles—his subtle one, full of heat and manly sex appeal that has my entire body buzzing.

"Then I think I'd be a pretty lucky woman."

"And he'd be a lucky man."

I stare up at him, wanting, waiting, hoping he'll kiss me—not for show, but for real. His eyes drop to my lips. I think he wants it too, but everything stops when his phone vibrates continuously in his pocket. His gaze breaks from my lips, shifting to my eyes. He doesn't move to answer. But the moment is ruined. The call severed all desire and pull between us.

He takes a step back, reaching into his pocket. "Sorry. Let me just silence it completely."

"It's okay if you want to answer." My eyes drop to the device just as he pulls it out. Calista James's face and name cover the screen, and it's like a cannonball blasts through my heart, leaving a perfectly hollow hole in the center.

"No, I don't need to answer. It can wait." He declines the call and switches the phone to silent, never noticing me seeing that it was Calista. Dropping the device back into his pocket, he looks up. "Come on. We better get back to Trey and Whitney." He glances at the circling speedboat twenty yards from the yacht. "I think we've given the paparazzi enough of a show."

"Definitely." I force a happy smile, but I'm stuck on Calista James and the word *show*.

CHAPTER
TWENTY-FIVE

CODY

THE FLIGHT ATTENDANT rushes back and forth down the aisle of the Flixmart plane, preparing for takeoff. I never know what they're checking or why they can't stay in one area, check all the things, then go to the other end of the plane and do the same thing. That seems like it would be much more efficient than the back and forth, but what do I know?

Jenna sits across from me with her eyes closed. She's not really asleep, just not into me. The last hour and a half of the wedding, while Trey and Whitney cut the cake and had their final dance, was like this. She's not rude or standoffish, just vacant, void of feeling toward me, which is a big change from where we were.

We almost kissed.

I *wanted* to kiss her, but I couldn't get past the dilemma in my mind. I can't give Jenna what she needs. Lasting relationships don't *last* when they're built around me. I'm the common denominator. I leave someone before they have the chance to leave me. What if I get scared and leave, breaking Jenna's heart like all the other men in her life? That's worst-case scenario. But even if I don't leave her, I can't get past the fear that Jenna will eventually realize I'm not good enough and walk away from me.

So I didn't kiss her when I had the chance.

Plus, there were so many nosy photographers with their long-range zoom lenses that it didn't seem like the right time to really kiss her the way I wanted.

And then the moment passed.

But I hate the emotional distance between us right now, so I try. "I really like your mom," I say, breaking out my pickaxe once again.

Her eyes open. "Yeah, she's really sweet. I didn't even know you'd talked to her."

"I spoke with both your parents before the wedding."

"Oh." She thinks about it for a second, mouth pushing downward. "You spoke with my dad too?"

"I didn't like your dad, so I thought I'd leave him out of this conversation."

Her brows rise in interest. "What didn't you like about my dad?"

"For starters, he called out me and my intentions toward you."

"I'm his baby girl." She shrugs. "Plus, he doesn't know about the fake relationship."

"I know. That's not the part I didn't like."

"Then what didn't you like?"

I scratch my forehead, hating that *this* is the conversation I struck up with her. Why didn't I break the ice with how beautiful she looked tonight, how much fun it was to dance with her, or basically anything else that doesn't have me throwing her father under the bus?

My hand drops, and I lean forward. "Have you ever noticed a similarity between the men you date and your dad?"

"No, not really."

"I'm noticing some patterns."

"Like what?"

Don't say it, Cody. Do not say it!

"Your dad is a chauvinistic jerk that treats your mother like she's a second-class citizen or some kind of trophy whose only value is how good she makes him look, and everyone just lets him get away with it instead of calling him out on his BS."

Shoot, I said it.

Jenna's lips press together in a slash as she takes in my words. "So you're saying I only date men that are chauvinistic jerks that treat me like I'm a second-class citizen or use me as the trophy on their arm?"

"Yes." My chest tightens, waiting for Jenna's wrath to fully unleash.

Instead, she nods and glances out the dark window to the tarmac.

"That's it?" I finally ask, watching her closely. "You don't have a comment or a complaint of my assessment?"

Her tired eyes shift to me.

"What do you want me to say, Cody? That I have terrible taste in men? That I always fall for the guy that never loves me back? That I'm going to end up unhappy and underappreciated like my mom?" She lifts her shoulders in the most defeated way. "You're right. I do all of that. And thanks to your assessment, I can pinpoint my bad choices in men back to my father. That information is helpful for the future, I guess. But it doesn't help me right now."

I'm a jerk.

"Jenna, I'm sorry. I shouldn't have said all that. I thought…" What did I even think? That telling her about her dad would somehow save her from ending up with some loser? "I don't know what I even thought. I should've just kept my mouth shut."

"It's fine." She shakes her head, looking back out the window. "It's been a long twenty-four hours. I think we're just tired. I'm too tired right now to figure out all my relationship problems and how they relate to my dad. I think I'll just save that deep dive for a therapist, you know?"

"Yeah, sure. That makes sense."

I still feel like a jerk. Like the absolute worst guy in the world. I don't think I could feel worse about how this night is ending.

Jenna's phone on the tray between us lights up with a text. She slowly leans forward, grabbing it. I watch her expression go from tired to hard as she reads it. Then her eyes flip to me.

I can't read the masked expression as she stares at me. I'm getting nothing, as if I've lost my internet connection in the middle of a search. Jenna is offline, and now the old-school dial-up ringtone plays in the back of my mind as each second ticks on.

"Is everything okay?"

She hands me the phone. "It's for you."

"For me? Why would a text to you be for me?" I take the device, watching as she immediately turns her gaze to the window again, like she couldn't care less what my reaction is.

Unknown Number: Hi, Jenna. This is Calista James. I got your number from your manager. I hope that's okay. I know it's super awkward that I'm texting you, but I've been trying to get ahold of Cody all night, and he isn't answering his phone. Maybe his battery died. You're with him at your brother's wedding, right? And just so you don't think I'm some homewrecker, I know your whole relationship is fake. Ha ha. Dallas and my manager have been working together on this to take the attention away from me and Cody while my divorce settles. Anyway, I was wondering if you could have Cody call me. I really need to talk to him. Thanks for your help! *kissy emoji*

"This isn't what you think," I immediately say.

"You don't have to explain anything to me." Her head shifts, and I wish she weren't such a good actor. I wish her eyes betrayed her right now, but they don't. They're absent of emotion. "She's your girlfriend. She's probably freaking out that she hasn't heard from you tonight. Give the poor woman a call."

"She's not my girlfriend. There's absolutely nothing romantic going on between us." I rub my beard, not knowing how I get myself in these kinds of situations. "Calista is just a friend. We worked together on my last movie when everything was going down with her marriage to Billie Francom. She opened up to me, and I sort of became her confidant. I can't tell you the details of her divorce because it's not my story to tell, but it's bad. All her other friends have turned on her and sided with Billie, so I'm all she has left. She just needs a friend and some occasional advice. That's all that's going on between us, but you know how the tabloids are. They take every relationship in my life and twist it into some sordid affair. But I swear, Jenna. I'm telling the truth."

The hardness that was once surrounding the edges of her eyes softens. "It's good she has a friend she can talk to." She glances at the phone. "You should call her. She must be having a really bad night."

"It can wait. I want to make sure everything between us is okay." I think about reaching for her, about grabbing her hand and lacing my fingers through hers to ease some of the tension I'm feeling, but I don't.

"There's nothing between us. Everything's fine. You should call Calista before we take off. I'm tired and will probably fall asleep on the flight anyway."

"Are you sure?"

She nods.

I hate just walking away, but Jenna has already leaned her head back and closed her eyes.

I don't think I'd get anything else from her even if I tried.

CHAPTER
TWENTY-SIX

JENNA

I BUILT a world out of glances across the room, longing stares, heated touches, and forbidden feelings.

I let myself fall in love with a dream.

Then it all blew up in my face. I'm left with the smell of smokey hair—figuratively speaking; my hair always smells great—and another broken heart.

"What happened when the wedding ended?" Winnie is sprawled out on my mattress, watching my stylist, Devon, twist my hair around a curling iron for the wrap party tonight.

"The yacht returned to the dock, a car took us to the airport, and we flew home." My demeanor, my voice, my *everything* is detached. I'm so detached from the Cody situation I'm like a garage on the side of a house.

Winnie flips to her stomach, resting her chin on her hands, swinging her feet in the air behind her. She looks like a six-year-old girl in pigtails with way too much enthusiasm for my Cody Banner story. I should probably tell her that love is a fantasy that only exists in movies. I know. I just filmed one of those fantasies that tricks young girls into believing that happily ever after exists.

But it doesn't exist.

"What about the plane ride?" she asks.

"Exactly." Devon pauses what he's doing with my hair and peeks at me. "You guys were alone together all night long. What happened then?"

"Nothing. We slept."

I don't bother telling them about Cody blaming my dad for all my stellar boyfriend choices—something that hadn't occurred to me before. I'm not mad about it. There's a lot of truth behind what he said. I can see it, but I don't have the energy or mental capacity right now to figure out what I'm going to do about it.

"But, like, you cuddled while you slept, right?" Winnie is too invested in this. Poor girl.

I lift my chin, keeping in line with my emotion-free exterior. "Why would we? There weren't any people or cameras around."

"Honey." Devon pats my shoulder. "Just because your relationship is for the public doesn't mean you can't take advantage of it in private."

"For real," Winnie adds.

My words are clipped. "We're just costars. Nothing more. Besides, he was on the phone with Calista James when I fell asleep."

"Oh," Devon mumbles as he picks up another strand of my hair.

Winnie's expression falls too, like they're both equally brokenhearted on my behalf.

"It's fine. Cody and Calista are just friends."

"And you actually believe that?" Devon asks.

The entire time I've known Cody, I've judged him based on what everyone in the media has said about him. But I know him now, and he has told me his side of the story. Am I going to trust in that or go back to believing everyone else?

236

I've decided I'd rather believe the person I know than the one I don't.

"Yeah, I believe that he and Calista are just friends. He hasn't given me a reason not to believe him."

Winnie sits up, crawling to the edge of the bed. "If they're just friends, let's forget about her and focus on you. What outfit are you wearing to the wrap party tonight?"

"I was thinking of the black-and-red dress." I nod toward where a dangerously short red leather dress with an overlay of black lace hangs in my closet. Black fringe on the hem and the cap sleeves add to the flirtiness. And don't even get me started on the scoop neckline that accentuates my collarbone and cleavage while leaving a lot of exposed skin. This jaw-dropping dress is my way of showing Cody exactly what he's missing.

Even though I believe he and Calista are just friends, and I'm not mad at him for what he said about my dad, I'm still hurt. He didn't kiss me last night when he had the chance. I know Calista called, but I'm talking about before that inter-ruption, when it was just the two of us gazing into each other's eyes.

It's not just about the kiss. I laid my heart on the line. I was more vulnerable with him than I've ever been, and he didn't say how he felt. He didn't say he wanted to be the man for me or that he was willing to try to make something real out of this relationship. I think that's what hurt the most. When everything was real for me, he was still putting on a show for the circling paparazzi.

"It's going to be a night to remember." Winnie claps, taking me out of my thoughts. "When Cody picks you up in forty-five minutes, he won't know what hit him."

Maybe. Or maybe he won't care because this is part of his job. And tonight, it's part of my job too, and I intend to work it like a teenager going out for employee of the month.

Tawny wants us to walk into the Gateway Club, where the

wrap party is being held, hand in hand. This is supposed to be an extension of a red-carpet event, so coming together and being photographed entering the club together was a big deal to her.

I mean, what's a good showmance without some red-carpet PDA?

CODY

JENNA LOOKS VERY nice in her black-and-red dress.

Very nice.

Who am I kidding? She knocks it out of the park in that thing.

I scrape my hands over my beard. It's going to be a long night. I'm already having a hard time keeping my eyes off her long legs every time we pass a streetlight. Those lamps create the perfect glow over her thighs. I need to stop thinking about her and her thighs, or else I'll pull my Jeep over, and well, there goes the wrap party.

I drag my stare back to the road. "Were you able to take a nap today?" I'm proud of my appropriate small talk. Although, I wouldn't have to conjure up small talk if Jenna were giving me any conversation of her own. But she's not.

"Yeah, I napped." Her head is turned away from me, eyes looking out the window.

"Me too. I was really tired. I'm hoping I can last at least a couple of hours here tonight." She doesn't respond. In fairness, I didn't ask a question, but usually, conversation has a bit more give and take than what I'm getting from her. "Hey, is everything alright?"

"Yep." Her eyes flip briefly to me as she answers, then shift back to the window.

"You seem a little off."

"Nope, I'm fine."

I scratch my head, glancing over her folded arms and closed-off body. Something is not right. I didn't expect her to hold my hand all the way to the club, but up until the end of the wedding last night, I was used to a little bit more from her. This feels like the beginning of our relationship, when we first started filming and she hated me.

I try one more time to get more out of her, because it's killing me to have so many walls between us. I don't think my heart has ever felt so uncomfortable in my entire life.

"Did I do something wrong?"

"Why would you think you did something wrong?"

"Well, there was the whole Calista thing—"

"Which I said I believed you on."

"Okay." I hesitate before listing another one of my crimes. "And then everything I said about your dad."

"I don't even care about that—at least, not right now."

I rub the back of my neck. "Then what is it?"

She stares at me again like I should know what I did.

What did I do?

I'm racking my brain and panicking all at the same time. Everything was fine. So fine that I wanted to kiss her, and then Calista called and interrupted things, and then we went back to the wedding party. I didn't notice at first that she was acting differently. Maybe she wasn't. There was a lot going on between the cake cutting and the bouquet toss.

Oh, man, maybe all of this is because Jenna didn't catch the bouquet. Women are sensitive about that kind of stuff, and I know how much she wants to get married.

"Is this about the bouquet?"

"What?" Her entire expression turns annoyed. This is definitely *not* about the bouquet. "That's dumb."

"Right. So dumb." Backpedal and agree. That's the strategy now.

"Don't worry." Her focus goes back to the window and whatever is more interesting than me. "I'll be fine in front of the cameras."

"I wasn't worried about the cameras. None of that matters to me."

We may have started this for show, but things changed for me. All I care about now is Jenna's well-being, and right now, nothing about her being seems *well*.

Silence fills the last few minutes of our car ride, and I hate it.

Hate it.

I pull up in front of the Gateway Club and glance at her as I shift the car into park. For three seconds, I try to come up with something to say to try and salvage the situation, but I'm drawing a blank.

My door opens, and a twenty-something valet driver stares at me. "Good evening, Mr. Banner."

Mr. Banner. I sound like an eleventh-grade history teacher.

"Hey." I drop out of the Jeep, handing him the keys.

The screaming fans lined up on the street go wild when they see me. I muster a smile even though I'm really distracted by everything that's happening with Jenna.

By the time I get to the passenger side of the car, security holds paparazzi and fans back. I open the door and take Jenna's hand, helping her decently get down from the tall Jeep without giving everyone a front-row show to whatever kind of underwear she has on under that skimpy dress. One mention of underwear and my heartbeat goes sporadic, but I'm not a weirdo. She's an underwear model—Jenna and sexy underwear are synonymous. I don't know why I added the sexy part. Maybe I am a weirdo. Moving on.

Jenna whips her head to the crowd, dazzling everyone with a giant, toothy smile. It's not her real one. No, I have that one memorized by heart, knowing every curve of her lips and lines at the corner of her eyes.

Camera lights flash like we're in old Hollywood, with the ancient popping and crackling bulbs blinding us. Jenna waves in slow motion and then glances up at me. The streetlight illuminates everything phony about her stare. There's no emotion behind her green eyes—okay, maybe there's a little indignation, but other than that, her gaze is void of everything I've grown to love about her.

"Cody! Jenna! Over here!"

She twists our bodies toward the cameras, trailing her hand to my neck. She keeps it there, tickling the back as more flashes go off. Nothing about her movement feels genuine. It's staged. So is the soft kiss she plants on my cheek.

My brows lower as she pulls back. "What are you doing?"

"Acting."

That one word hits me across the face like a back-handed slap, which hurts more and leaves a longer sting, but she doesn't keep her eyes on me long enough to even see my reaction. Instead, she turns back to the cameras, leading me down the sidewalk.

Hand in hand, we walk to the step-and-repeat backdrop that has the Flixmart and *The Promised Prince* logos printed all over it. Jenna curls into my side, an action that I'd normally welcome, but today it feels wrong. She's leaning, pressing, grabbing, and touching me, but it's all so overdone and without feeling it makes my stomach sick.

But I smile, keeping our angles and where we look the same. Jenna's hand slides down my body to the dip above my backside, gazing up at me with another one of her excessive smiles. Basically, her hand is on the top of my butt, which should be a good thing, especially since this is the first time it's ever been there. But I can't even enjoy it because I know it's not real. She's not touching me this way because she wants to. It's all a facade.

"Kiss! Kiss!" one photographer yells, and before I can pull away, Jenna's lips are on top of mine, but this kiss is nothing like the one we shared a few days ago. This kiss is bland and forced.

More flashes. More pictures.

Everyone gets what they want.

The photographers get their magazine spread.

The doting fans get a happily ever after.

Dallas gets to say he fixed the infamous bad boy's reputation.

Tawny gets Jenna's acting career off the ground.

Quinton gets his ratings up.

And me and Jenna? Do either of us actually get what we want?

All I know is that I don't want this.

CHAPTER
TWENTY-SEVEN

JENNA

ONCE INSIDE THE club and away from the cameras, I pull my fingers out of Cody's grasp. He looks back, eyeing my now empty hand. Hurt radiates from his stare, but he doesn't say anything. He turns and keeps walking toward the back of the club, where some of the cast sit at a giant round booth.

"Hey!" the entire table cheers when we approach.

"Look who it is!" Teague stands, pulling Cody into one of those bro hugs, while I take the opportunity to slide into a seat, scooting way over.

"You're all in a good mood." I pick up someone's half-empty glass, not knowing what kind of drink it's filled with, and gulp it down, swallowing hard as the sting of alcohol coats my throat.

"Of course we're in a good mood." Teague sits next to me before Cody can scoot in. I feel his eyes on me but don't meet his stare. "Haven't you heard the good news?"

"What good news?" Cody mutters, taking the seat across from me.

"Flixmart signed us for season two. We'll start pre-production on *The Stolen Princess* this fall." Teague lifts his glass, and everyone does the same, clanking them together in the middle.

I grab the glass out of Kylee's hand and drink it before she has the chance.

"Yikes, Jenna," she says. "Slow down. The night is young."

I wince from the burn in my throat and push a smile onto my lips. "I'm just happy, right? We did it. We signed season two." My eyes gravitate to Cody, but they don't linger. The last thing I want is for him to notice my disappointment.

I shouldn't be disappointed. Season two is what we wanted, what we've been working toward with the ratings. But the heaviness in my chest weighs me down like I'm a thousand feet underwater with no oxygen.

It's over. Everything between Cody and me is all over.

Actually, it was over last night, the second I laid my heart on the line, and he left it dangling there.

I should be glad the contract states this fake relationship ends when the ratings go up and Flixmart signs season two. I *am* glad. Now I can just move on with my life and forget that this whole Cody Banner thing ever existed.

I leave for Milan tomorrow to do a photoshoot. It's not something I was planning on or even going to do, but after everything that happened last night between Cody and me, I thought some space was a good idea. So I called Tawny and told her I was in. The timing works out perfectly.

Everyone talks around me, chatting about celebrity gossip and rumors of who will be cast in the next season. I sit back against the leather bench, only moving to take a drink from the waitress's tray when she brings another round.

"Jenna?" Cody says over the noise and music. "Jenna?" My eyes flip to him, but I don't say anything. "Can we talk?"

"We are talking." I look around the table.

"I mean in private."

I should say no, except that would be really rude, and

there's still a part of me that longs to hear what he has to say. That's the freaking hope part.

"Okay." The relief that washes over his face is endearing.

CODY

I LEAD Jenna through the crowd to the VIP section in the back.

A security guard steps in front of us. "This area is off limits."

"We just need a second."

The guard's eyes drift to her, and a flicker of recognition passes through them. There it is again. Another person who recognizes her and not me, and I don't even care. How could you ever forget a woman like Jenna? His eyes rove over her body, and I seriously contemplate putting him in a headlock. Can you put security guards in headlocks? Luckily, I don't need to test it out because he whips open the curtain, letting us go through.

"Just for a moment, Miss Lewis."

"Thanks." She walks to the back of the room by the table, spinning to face me.

I called this meeting, so I decide to go first. "What's your deal tonight?"

"Nothing."

"That crap you pulled out front when we came in the club wasn't nothing."

"I was just packing on the PDA for the cameras. Isn't that what you do?"

"No. When it comes to you and me, I've never done anything I didn't want to do."

"Isn't that the truth?" It's not so much a question, more like a bitter statement.

The hurt behind her voice takes me by surprise, and I take a step toward her, softening. "Jenna, tell me what's wrong. What changed?"

"Nothing changed." She looks at me, blinking back the beginnings of tears. "This is fake. It's only ever been fake. When it was real for me, it wasn't for you. Which is fine. You don't have to—"

"What are you even talking about?"

"Last night at the wedding. I thought I made it pretty clear that I was talking about you and me, and it seemed like you were too, but then it just stopped. Nothing happened." Her shoulders lift. "You didn't say anything more, and you didn't kiss me, and it's fine. You don't have to feel any of that or even want to kiss me. We're just acting, right?"

"You think I didn't want to kiss you?"

"Listen, we don't have to go through this whole thing. It's fine."

"I *wanted* to kiss you, but I'm trying to do the right thing. I'm trying to be a good guy here."

"I don't need you to be a good guy for me."

"I know that, but I *want* to be a good guy for you. I want to show you what it's like to have a man who respects and adores you. You deserve more than the losers you keep dating, and when you finally have a guy in front of you who does the right thing and doesn't kiss you, you're mad at him."

Her brows pull together. "How is not kissing me doing the right thing?"

"There were a ton of paparazzi around. You deserve something more special than that. A kiss with you shouldn't happen because it's written in a script, or because someone tells you it will improve ratings for a show, or because some sleazy photographer needs a good shot." I cup my hands on her cheeks. "When I kiss you, you shouldn't doubt whether or not it's real. You should know I'm doing it because I want to."

Her green eyes scan mine. "Do you want to?"

"I've literally never wanted anything more in my entire life."

"Then kiss me." Heat and desire crackle between us as her voice lowers to a whisper. "Then kiss me, Cody."

I don't hesitate.

I pull Jenna in. Or maybe she pulls me in. The specifics of how we ended up with our mouths and our bodies pressed together are unknown.

We skip the polite kissing and go straight to the I'm-desperate-for-you kissing. That wasn't originally part of my plan. I had no plan, but here we are, colliding into the table against the wall in the VIP room at Gateway Club.

There are a few minutes of fumbling and kissing until Jenna rises to her toes. I take the signal and lift her up so she's sitting on the table while I explore her body with my hands and her lips with mine. I never knew multitasking was such a strength of mine, but in this moment, I'm killing it.

Jenna sits back, tipping over empty wine glasses, ruining the table presentation. I follow, trying not to stop our feverish momentum. She tosses table settings and plates aside while still kissing me. She's a great multitasker as well. Once a spot has been cleared, she lies back, dragging my body on top of hers.

If we were restrained before, we're not now.

Jenna's fingers dig through my hair as I kiss her mouth and neck. My hand travels over her smooth leg—I've never loved a short dress so much in my life as I do in this moment. Surely, whoever came up with that design is a passionate man, like I am right now.

There's no more acting or fictional pretenses. We're both feeling the connection.

Things are getting good.

Too good.

But somewhere in the back of my mind, the upstanding version of myself, the version that wants to be the kind of man who deserves a woman like Jenna Lewis, knocks me into reality.

Jenna is worth more than an impassioned moment in a VIP lounge at a wrap party.

I want more for her than that.

I want to be more than that.

Half of me hopes I can, hopes someone like her would choose someone like me despite all my past mistakes. But the other half knows I can't give her what she wants. Not fully.

I break the kiss, letting out the most frustrated breath of my life.

Her green eyes search mine. "What is it?"

Her breathy voice is enough to make me want to throw all my morals out the window, but I don't. I crawl backward off her body until my feet hit the ground.

Jenna leans up on her elbows. "Are you okay?"

My eyes drift to her beautiful face and her lips. "I just got done telling you that you deserve the best, and then I do this."

Her smile is sultry. "I wish you'd do more."

Dang, this woman can be a temptress when she wants to be.

I push my hands through my hair. "We need to leave, or else I won't be able to stop myself."

She laughs, amused by my struggle. "Cody Banner, the playboy, knows when to draw the line."

"It looks like it."

"Wait until the tabloids hear about this. Your entire bad-boy reputation will go up in flames."

I honestly wish it would, and I wish Jenna were the reason for it.

"Come on." I reach my hand out to her, pulling her up to

her feet. She straightens her dress and her hair, making sure everything looks normal. "Let's get back to the party."

I tug her forward, but her feet stop. "Cody?" I turn over my shoulder, glancing at her. "They signed season two."

"I know."

"That's supposed to be the end of the fake relationship."

I smile back at her in a teasing way. "It doesn't have to be."

Her expression goes serious. "What does that mean?"

"Just that, it doesn't have to be the end. We can keep playing the relationship up for the cameras and finish out each episode's release with a bang."

"And then what?"

I lift my shoulders but don't answer. I know I like Jenna *a lot*—more than any other woman I've ever been with. I know I don't want to lose her, but that's where my answers stop.

It's not that I don't believe in love, because I do. I believe that two people can have strong feelings and desires. It's what happens after those feelings fade that scares me. I've convinced myself my entire life that I've already lived through the emotional damage that comes from the aftermath of love. I don't want to do it again.

So even though I have a tangible feeling for Jenna that I've only ever heard described, not actually experienced myself, I'm not sure I can see it through all the way. I could never give her the one thing she wants. I could never marry her.

"Cody, what happens after the fake relationship and all the acting is over?" she presses.

"I…I don't know. Maybe we can just give it some time and figure it out later."

She stares back at me, nodding over and over while she thinks. Her hand drops out of mine, and she takes a step back. "I'm tired. I think I'm just going to go home for the night."

"No, don't leave like this." I put my hands on her waist, as if I can make her stay. "Come back in the club with me."

Her chin lifts, not in defiance but to really look in my eyes. "As what? Your friend? Your costar? Your fake girl-friend? Your real girlfriend? Your lover? What would I be, Cody?"

I'm caught off guard by the question and the implications. I want to give Jenna the answer she's looking for, reassure her that there's this magical future between us. But I can't. And I won't do what countless other men have done—play with her heart until the whistle blows and the game is over. She means too much to me.

So I settle for shaking my head and shrugging, the worst possible answer a man could ever give a woman.

Jenna's expression masks over. "When we were at the table, I already texted a car to pick me up. I think I'm just going to head home." She squeezes my arm and then walks past me.

"Jenna, wait." I say the words, but my feet don't move. I can't promise her what she wants to hear, but it's killing me not to chase after her.

I say I want to grow up.

I say that I want to change.

But what if I really don't? What if I keep sabotaging rela-tionships because I want to be alone for the rest of my life?

JENNA

I EXIT out the back of the club. My driver leans against the side of his car but straightens when he sees me.

"Miss Lewis." He nods as he holds the car door open for me.

"Hi, Michael." I move to climb inside but stop when I hear Cody's voice.

"Jenna, wait!"

His steps are rushed as he runs to me, and I seriously want to fire my treacherous heart for being so excited that he came after me. Like, whose side are you on, anyway?

"Don't go. Not like this." Cody holds the door, boxing out Michael until he gets the point and walks around to his side of the car.

"Like what?" This will be the performance of my lifetime. He can never know how much his indifference hurt me. I shrug, mustering the best smile my broken soul can manage. "I'm fine, Cody. I'm just tired. We've been running like crazy and just got home early this morning from Tampa. I'm going to go home and sleep."

"See, and I think you're leaving because I didn't answer your question back there. It's not that I didn't want to answer it; I just couldn't. This isn't me being classic 'Cody Banner.'" He puts his name in air quotes. "I'm not playing games or anything like that. I just don't want to promise you something I can't follow through on."

I know.

I've *always* known that at the end of this, when the series promotion and the fake relationship are over and done, Cody and I would end. It might not be for the reasons I originally thought. I no longer think he's some player intentionally messing with my feelings for the sport of it. He's just not built for relationships or marriage. A man incapable of giving love a chance, pre-wired for a life of singlehood. He told me himself back in Malibu.

I've known all along.

I tried to protect myself from it but failed miserably.

He broke my heart, but not because he wanted to or meant to.

It's just what happened.

I can stick around and keep letting it happen until we've gone too far down that path, or I can end things now.

"I know," I say with a sad smile, placing my hand on his chest. "And I still want more. So let's just call it what it is: a fake relationship that, for a moment, got a little too real."

He places his hand on top of mine, holding both against his body. "It's more than that."

The fact that it was more to him is a little consoling. A broken heart over something real sits a lot better than a broken heart over something fake.

So I'll take my consolation prize and leave with my head held high.

I smile big. "I had a lot of fun with you. You really are a great guy, Cody. Don't let the media tell you otherwise." I lean onto my toes, placing a soft kiss on his cheek. "I'll see you soon, okay?" I slip my fingers out from under his hand and drop into the car. He doesn't hold the door, just lets me close it. "Let's go, Michael."

The car slowly pulls away as I watch Cody stand on the curb with his hand still pressed over his heart.

We make it about ten feet when the tears start. I press my head against the seat and close my eyes as teardrop after teardrop rolls down each side of my face, curling over my jawline and continuing onto my chest.

Why does this keep happening to me?

CHAPTER
TWENTY-EIGHT

JENNA

THE WING of the airplane slices through some clouds as I look out the window.

It looks like I'm running.

I'm not running.

I'm going to Milan for a photoshoot. The timing just happens to perfectly align with my need for space from Cody. But since I never told him I was leaving town, it really does look like I'm running.

This whole thing is my fault. I complicated everything by not just acting. I knew better, and now I'm paying the price for it.

Tawny sits across from me with a laptop out on the table between us. "People are going wild over the pictures of you and Cody from Trey's wedding and the wrap party last night." She spins the laptop in front of me so I can see the pictures, even though I never asked to see them. The first one is of us on the yacht before the moment when I thought he would kiss me. Our hands are all over each other, and genuine smiles cover both of our faces.

"I can't see it. The sun's glare is bad." What a little liar

I am.

Tawny frowns, trying to peek around the screen, but gives up. "You can look at them later 'cause they're fabulous." She turns the screen back to herself. "I don't think you two could be in more demand than you are now." The click of her mouse keeps my attention, even though I just want to go back to daydreaming out the window. "Speaking of demand. I've received several requests for you to come read for some new roles. One with Flixmart, which I'm sure you're a shoo-in for, and then two movies. I think we should consider and prepare for the movies to really capitalize on the fake-relationship popularity."

"How much longer do we need to keep up the fake relationship?"

"The contract says until the ratings go up and Flixmart signs on season two."

"And that's already happened."

"The fake relationship isn't hurting anything. Maybe we should let it go a little longer, ride it until the end."

I shift my eyes back to the window, not liking the answer I knew she would give me.

My phone vibrates in my hand, and I glance down. Cody's profile picture covers the entire screen. He's calling me. Nobody calls anyone anymore. There's a blip in my heartbeat at the prospect of how fun it would be to talk to Cody on the phone. Okay, it's more than a blip. It's a freaking Olympic high jump. I click the button on the side of my phone, darkening the screen, and return my hands back to my lap.

"Who was that?" Tawny asks, barely looking up from what she's working on.

I shake my head. "Nobody important."

Another lie. Cody Banner is important to me.

My phone buzzes again. If Hollywood's biggest playboy left me an old-fashioned voicemail, I would be instantly turned off by him. I don't do voicemails.

I flip the phone over again.

Cody: Hey, can I come over? I just want to talk. See if you're okay after everything last night.

Right now, I'm seriously cursing the in-flight Wi-Fi. Everything would be so much easier if I could completely disconnect from Cody physically, mentally, and cellularly—if that's even a word.

I close out of the text, giving myself some time to think about my response. I need to keep my story in line with what I said last night. Cody can never know the extent of my heartbreak. If he knows, he'll feel guilty—an emotion he doesn't deserve since, from the beginning, he's been nothing but honest with me about who he is and what he wants.

But worse than that, if he knows how sad I am, he might try to stay, try to give me more than he's capable of, and I can't ask him to do that. I want him, but not for the wrong reasons.

So I open my phone back up.

Jenna: Hey! I'm so much better after a little sleep and a clear head. I think I might've been a little buzzed. I wish we could get together, but I just left for Milan. I have a photoshoot there. Sorry.

I left out my return date or any mention of plans when I get home. And I added that I might've been a little drunk. I feel like that helps strengthen my whole *I'm fine* case.

Cody: You left?

Jenna: Yeah, didn't I tell you about it?

I definitely did not tell him about it.

255

Cody: No. I would've remembered. When do you get back?

I think about fudging the dates but decide, since I've already lied so much about my "fine" emotional state, honesty is probably best at this point.

Jenna: I'll be here for a week.

Cody: Can I call you right now?

Jenna: Service in the air isn't that great. I tried answering your call, but it didn't go through.

How quickly I've turned again to my lying ways.

Cody: Okay, what about tonight? Can I call you then?

Jenna: I'll be working.

My fingers pause over the keyboard, contemplating my next thought.

Jenna: And what good would talking do? We're kind of at a standstill, don't you think? Let's just cut our losses before anything more happens. I told you last night. I'm fine.

Cody: But I'm not fine.

Those words equally melt and hurt my heart at the same time.

Jenna: This is Cody Banner we're talking about. You're going to be just fine. Give it a few days.

Cody: What if I don't want to give it a few days?

Jenna: It doesn't matter. I want to give it a few days.

Cody: Okay, I can respect that. We'll give it a week while you're in Milan and talk when you get home.

Jenna: Sure. I'll text you when I get back.

I'm absolutely *not* texting him when I get home.

Cody: Jenna, I miss you.

Not enough to love me.

I click off the phone and continue my in-depth analysis of the clouds out my window.

"Okay, do you want me to set up a reading for those movie parts?" Tawny looks at me expectantly.

"Sure." I nod. "And I also want you to prepare the Cody Banner amicable breakup story to go public the day I get home from Milan."

"Jenna," Tawny pouts. "I think you're making a mistake. My professional opinion is that you should keep this fake relationship going, at least until you get one of the roles in the movie."

"And what if I don't get the movie role? Then what? How long do we let this charade keep going?"

"Until it no longer benefits us."

"That's where I'm at right now. Being in a relationship with Cody doesn't benefit me." I glance back to the window. "Make the breakup happen."

Tawny sulks into her chair but doesn't say anything, which is good because, despite her tantrum, I'm not changing my mind about ending this fake relationship.

CHAPTER
TWENTY-NINE

CODY

EVERYONE CAN COUNT TO FIVE. It's the first
number sequence a child learns. It's how many fingers are on
a hand (I'm including the thumb). And it's the number of days
it's been since I've talked to Jenna. Suddenly, five feels like the
biggest number ever created.

I'm struggling.

I ate a double bacon cheeseburger and then didn't work
out for two days. My showers are no longer showers but afternoon events until the hot water turns cold. And the first three
episodes of *The Promised Prince* play on repeat at my house.
Episode four comes out tomorrow, so obviously, I'll be busy
watching that all day, over and over.

I've written a dozen speech texts to Jenna this week but
erased them all before pushing send. I'm trying to give her
space while also trying to figure out what I want.

It shouldn't be this hard to know what you want.

I park my Jeep in an open spot on the street in LA and
hop out of the car, pulling my hat down over my face and
sunglasses.

I'm meeting Dallas for lunch to discuss the next steps in

my career. I have a side role in a movie set to begin filming this fall, and when you combine that with my small appearance in season two, *The Stolen Princess*, it's enough to keep me busy for the next few months.

This meeting is to talk about what comes after that. With my recent uprising in likability and popularity—thanks to Jenna—the movie roles are pouring in. And not just roles, *big* roles being offered to me over big names in Hollywood. Everyone is clamoring for a piece of Cody Banner. I've never been this in-demand before. I should be ecstatic about my change in circumstances, but I can't even seem to fake a smile about it.

My career is at an all-time high while my personal life is in shambles.

I've always been the guy who walks away from a relationship and doesn't look back. But everything is different with Jenna. She walked away from me. She said she didn't want to talk to me. And I'm scared that she's just going to be another person in my life who's going to leave me for good because I don't bring any value to them. I want to add value. I want to add to her life in a way that no one else can. I just need help. I need someone to show me *how* to get over all my fears.

I walk inside the restaurant and immediately spot Dallas. He lifts his finger, signaling to me.

"Sorry I'm late. I was watching…" My words drift once I realize that admitting to my favorite pastime, watching Jenna and me together in *The Promised Prince,* is embarrassing. "I was watching boxing." Yeah, that sounds manly, not like a lovesick, sappy fool.

"Boxing? In the middle of the day?"

"Yeah, reruns from the fight." I have no clue when the last big match was. "The one a couple of months ago. Crazy stuff. I got lost in it."

"Who won?"

Is Dallas seriously a fan?

"The guy." I roll my fingers over and over. "You know, the guy that always wins."

"Terence Crawford?"

Are you kidding me? Dallas really is a fan.

"Yep." I point at him. "That's the one."

"You know, he has twenty-nine knockouts."

More importantly, why does Dallas know that stat off the top of his head?

"Yeah. But we didn't come here to talk about that. Let's get to your news." I take a sip of the water in front of me.

"First things first, I made a few phone calls, and I have a meeting set up with a top divorce attorney in LA that's been trying to do some work for kids caught in custody battles. She's excited to talk with you and discuss some options and ways you can help those kids out."

"That's great, right?"

"Yeah, if that's what you want to do, then she'll have the contacts to help you get started."

"Thank you. That's perfect. I've been wondering about that."

"Next, we have a lot of movie roles to wade through. What did you think about the thriller script I sent you?"

I shake my head.

"What about the script for the action movie where you're the villain who—"

"No." I shake my head again.

"You usually like playing the villain."

"I don't know. I'm just not feeling it right now. What about the one with the kid?"

Dallas's brows hike. "You're talking about the one where you'd play the part of the single dad who falls in love with his son's second-grade teacher?"

"Yeah, that one."

"Out of all the scripts I gave you, that's the role you want to go for?" I don't know why Dallas looks so surprised. He's the one that wanted me to start portraying more mature characters.

"Yeah, the script was funny and emotional. I liked the heart and the message behind it." I take a sip of my water.

"Okay, then. We'll go for the single-dad role." Dallas makes a note on his phone before looking back up at me. "Last thing, Tawny is going to release a statement on Friday that you and Jenna decided to part ways—a mutual, amicable decision."

Water spits out of my mouth with so much force it showers Dallas.

"What?" I try helping him dry off with my napkin. "Why would she do that?"

His lips push into a frown as he wipes his shirt with his own napkin. "I know. I don't love it either, but Jenna's camp is firm on this."

"But why?"

"They say the fake relationship ran its course, and since the terms of the contract have been met, there's nothing I can do."

The relationship did *not* run its course. We're on mile two, with a full marathon ahead. Right now is like a bathroom break before we get things moving again.

"But I think we can still capitalize on your connection to Jenna. I'll throw out a few rumors that you're still together in a week or two. Maybe leak some pictures from Malibu that we didn't use. You know, the typical stuff to keep the momentum going for us."

"You said Jenna's camp is firm on this?"

"Yes, but like I said, we'll make it work." Dallas studies me for a second. "Why do you look like you just got hit by a truck? I thought you'd be happy about this."

I lean my elbows on the table, resting my head against my palms. "I don't want to break up with Jenna. I like her."

"She's very nice, but these showmances usually fizzle out, and you can remain friends."

"No, I *like* her…more than a friend."

"Like, for real?"

I nod my head up and down.

"Wait. You and Jenna. For real?"

I lift my head, giving him a pointed look. "Why is that so hard to believe?"

"Because you're Cody Banner." He gestures to me. "You hired me to fix your playboy reputation, because your past relationships all had a shelf life of three weeks, so I'm just having a hard time wrapping my head around this whole thing."

"Maybe I don't want to do that anymore. Maybe it's finally time to grow up."

"Do you love her?"

I look away, zeroing in on a waiter across the restaurant.

"Oh, boy." Dallas sits back in his chair with a giant smile. "You love her."

"I never said that."

"Then what, Cody? What do you want with her?"

"I don't know. I've been trying to figure that out."

"Jenna Lewis is a sweet girl. She's not like the other women you've been rumored with. You don't toy around with a woman like her. She's the kind you settle down with."

"You think I don't know that?"

"If you know that, then I'll ask my question again. What do you want with her? Where do you see your relationship in five years?"

Jenna said marriage and kids are part of her five-year plan —things that have never been on any plan of mine, let alone a five-year one.

"I don't know."

"That's not an answer. You're the only person who can know."

"I know what I want, but it doesn't exist."

"Okay, let's start there. Tell me what you want."

"I want Jenna in real life, but I also don't want to commit to anything. I want us to be together and for her to be okay with the fact that I'm not promising marriage or forever. I want all of that to be enough for her."

Dallas picks up his napkin and throws it at me, disgusted.

"Did you really just throw a napkin at me?"

"Yes, I did."

"Why?" I crumple it up and throw it back.

"Because your answer sucks."

"It doesn't suck. It was honest. You told me to start with what I wanted that doesn't exist, so I did."

"Not once did you ever mention what Jenna wants."

"That's because you asked what *I* wanted. You should've phrased the question differently if you wanted a different answer. You should've said, 'What does Jenna want?'"

"Do you even know what Jenna wants?"

"I have a pretty good idea, and what she wants doesn't align with what I want."

"If you really love someone, then what you want becomes irrelevant. Their wants become your wants. Meeting their needs becomes your life goal. In return, they'll do the same for you. They'll bend over backward to make sure you're happy. That's what true and selfless love is—that's the ultimate goal. Labels like marriage and happily ever after don't mean anything. It's just an avenue, a way to create a lasting relationship where selflessness can grow."

"So maybe I don't *actually* love Jenna." There's a little bit of relief, like this new realization will somehow ease the ache I've been carrying around ever since she left me on the curb at the nightclub. "You said yourself that I was only thinking about what I wanted. Jenna wants to get married and have children, and I think I'd do that for her. I'd throw all my hesitations and pessimistic beliefs out the window just to be with her. But I'm worried that, at the last second, after I've promised her the fairy tale, I'd chicken out and leave. And I don't want to do that to her. I don't want to lead her on and break her heart when we both realize I'm not the man she deserves. I don't want to do that because—"

"Because you *love* her." A goofy grin spreads across his mouth.

"No." I shake my head. "I was just saying why I thought I *didn't* love her."

"Cody, if you're willing to walk away from her just so she has a chance at real happiness, then you love her. Love requires sacrifice, putting your partner above everything else. You're willing to do that for Jenna."

"I am?"

"You're willing to walk away from her even though you don't want to, right?"

"Well, yeah, but—"

"Then you passed the test. You love her."

"Okay, but love is not enough."

"But the willingness to sacrifice is. That's what I'm trying to explain to you."

This all feels very complicated.

"I don't know." I sigh. "I just don't think it's smart for me to commit to something I don't even believe in."

Dallas's eyes show disappointment. "Cody, I thought you finally wanted to grow up."

"I do."

I think.

I say I do, but what if I don't really mean it? What if I like pushing people away, using my parents as justification for my immaturity?

"Stop running from everything you're scared of. If you love Jenna, go after her. If you want to be with her, be with her. If you want a marriage to last, fight for it. You and Jenna decide how this all ends. The effort you put in is what makes it last. So grow up and put the effort in."

Look at Mr. L.L. Bean coming in strong with advice on love. I thought I hired Dallas to make me likable, but maybe I hired him to be my relationship coach. If this whole publicity thing doesn't work out for him, he definitely has a future in love and relationship therapy.

I suck in a deep breath. "I want to put the effort in, but I think we might be too late. If Jenna is initiating this breakup, then she's already decided she wants nothing to do with me."

"And you're just going to accept that?"

"Well…" My shoulders sink. "I don't know what else to do."

"Are you a man? Or are you a man?"

"Is that a trick question?"

He picks up his phone in exasperation.

I lean in, trying to get a glimpse of his screen. "What are you doing?"

"I'm texting Tawny and telling her not to leak the breakup story."

I point to his phone. "Good idea. We're not breaking up. We're sticking this relationship out for better or worse. I'm not letting Jenna get rid of me." But I'm at a disadvantage because I have no clue when she's coming home. I point to Dallas's phone again. "Can you also find out from Tawny when Jenna's flight gets in? She said we could talk when she gets home, so I'm going to show up at her house and tell her…" I pause because saying these words feel big. "I guess I'm going to tell her I love her."

"That's the spirit." Dallas gives an approving nod.

I love Jenna.

It's crazy, and exciting, and completely scares me.

But it is what it is. I love her and can't live without her, so I better start figuring out how to get over my fears about marriage so I can be the man she deserves.

THAT NIGHT after lunch with Dallas and all the personal strides I've made with my own feelings, I sit down to send Jenna a text. I've erased and rewritten, erased and rewritten, but I finally think I've come up with the perfect text to send to her:

Cody: Fine. I can admit that Jenna Lewis has the most exquisite legs, butt, and chest I've ever seen. I don't need to zoom in on a picture to know that. I've witnessed it firsthand. And I can also admit that, yes, I'm falling for her sweet, caring, intelligent, multi-talented, number-counting mind. And I already know whether or not she's a good kisser in real life and in front of the cameras. But I also know that I miss her and can't live without her.

I push send, hoping that my imitation text comes across as cute, not cringy. But once it's gone, I panic.

I cannot believe I just sent that.

I think it might be cringy.

Should I delete it?

I should probably delete it before Jenna has the chance to read it.

But then I see the little 'read' sign at the bottom of the text. There's no turning back now. I wait for the dots. There are no dots. Why are there no dots?

For the next two hours, I drive myself crazy, checking my phone every two seconds just in case I've missed her response.

I haven't.

Because she doesn't respond.

Crap. Convincing her I'm the one for her is going to be harder than I thought.

CHAPTER
THIRTY

CODY

MY JEEP IS SUSPICIOUSLY PARKED around the corner from Jenna's house. But that's how it has to be for the element of surprise. Showing up at her house unannounced is my love gesture. Every good romance movie has one. Heck, *The Promised Prince* has two.

So this is what I'm doing.

I'm going to sit on her front porch until she gets home.

The only problem is, I can't get over the walls around her property to get to her front porch. I walk back and forth, assessing each bush, looking for a point of access where I can enter. There's nothing. I guess that's a good thing. I'd rather Jenna be safe than have an easy place for some creep to get over her walls.

Some creep like me.

I think if I just climb up the gate where cars enter, I can swing my legs over the top and hop to the other side. It's a really tall gate—like, twelve feet tall. So I get a running start and scale it until my hands reach the top.

If I'm being honest, it took me three tries. But just for my ego, let's say I got ahold of the top of the gate the first time.

My body dangles, hanging with arms extended, until I use my upper-body strength to pull myself up so I'm straddling the gate with a leg on either side. Sweat gathers at the base of my hairline. Not ideal timing. No man wants to confess his love to a woman when he's a sweaty mess. I wipe what I can with my sleeve, hoping by the time Jenna gets here, I'll be a little more poised.

The gate unlocks. There's a sudden humming sound and a jerk of movement. My butt travels backward. I glance behind me in full-on panic mode, watching the gate disappear inside the looming wall. Headlights turn into the drive, stopping in front of the moving rail, but I don't have any time to think about how stupid it is that Jenna arrived home in the middle of my property break-in. I just need to get off this gate before there isn't any gate left.

I swing my leg around and leap off. I could've planned my fall better, especially since I end up landing on top of Jenna's car. My body hits the hood with a thud.

"That's going to leave a dent," I groan.

"Cody?" Jenna is out of the car, standing next to me. "What are you doing?"

"Climbing your gate so I could meet you on your front porch." I slide off the car, trying not to wince or hold any of the dinged-up places on my body. I still have an image to uphold—I haven't won the girl yet.

"Are you okay?" She grabs my arm, and it's so nice to see her, to feel her touch. I study her face instead of answering.

"Cody? Are you hurt?" Her words are slow, as if she thinks I have a concussion.

"Yeah, I'm fine." I hold my side against my better judgment. "You? How are you?"

She squints, shaking her head at me, and suddenly, nothing about this plan feels like a good idea, even apart from riding her moving gate.

"Miss Lewis, is everything okay?" The driver looks back and forth between us.

"Yes, Michael. Thank you." She turns to him. "You can just take my luggage up to the door and then head home."

He nods and climbs back in the driver's seat. We step to the side as the car rolls past us into Jenna's driveway and flips around.

"So what are you doing here?"

We begin a slow walk up her drive.

"We said we'd talk when you got home."

"Not *right* when I got home. I said I'd text you."

"It couldn't wait."

She slows to a stop. "If this is about the amicable breakup. It's too late. Tawny already sent the information out."

"What?" I throw my hands up. "I told Dallas to tell her not to do that."

"I told her to do it anyway."

"So we're broken up?"

"Yes."

"Come on!" I kick my foot as if there's an imaginary ball that I want to launch over the wall I just fell off of. I glance at Michael, the driver, who's slowly placing luggage on her porch as if he wants to see how my temper tantrum plays out. None of this is the romantic gesture I had in my mind.

"Cody, I'm tired and have jetlag, so can we just talk about this tomorrow?"

I didn't calculate jetlag into the equation. That seems like something I should've thought about.

"I don't know." I throw my arms up, frustrated by how bad this is all going. "I didn't show up here to talk about the breakup, but whatever. I'll just come back tomorrow." I spin like I'm going to leave.

"I got your text."

I about-face so fast I'd put any soldier to shame.

"You did? I mean, I know you did, but you didn't text me back, so I didn't know what you thought about it."

Her expression softens, giving me some encouragement. "I thought it was cute."

My lips lift. "I hoped it was cute."

"It was cute."

Michael has stalled long enough, and with no other luggage to carry up to Jenna's porch, he climbs in the car. We watch as the vehicle slowly rolls forward, and I've never been so happy to wave goodbye to someone in my entire life.

When his taillights round the corner, I turn to Jenna. "Real or fake?"

"What?"

"Was the connection between us real or fake? For you? I know you didn't like me at first, and everything about me repulsed you, and I was the last man on earth that you'd ever want to be with, but—"

"Cody, I was never repulsed by you."

"I have several months of memories that prove otherwise."

She laughs, shaking her head. "That's just what I had to do to protect my heart. When it came to my feelings for you, it was always the opposite. I pushed you away because I knew that the second I let you in, I'd completely fall for you. You're everything that I can't stay away from."

"That sounds more like a bad thing than a good thing, but I'm choosing to spin it into a positive and go back to my first question because everything else I have to say depends on your answer." I look deep into her eyes. "Real or fake?"

"Real." She shrugs.

"Same." I take a step forward, trying to keep my smile in check. That was only the first hurdle of many that I need to get over. "While in a fake relationship with Jenna Lewis, I fell for her: real."

"Cody, it's not really about whether or not our feelings are legit. It's about what happens next if they are. A relationship between us doesn't make sense. We both want different things."

"I've thought a lot about that." I hold my finger up like I have a really valid point to make. "And I think I can meet you halfway."

"I don't want halfway. I want the entire fantasy."

"If that's what you want, then that's what I want too. I just don't want to lose you."

"And I don't want you to completely change something about yourself just because of me."

"That's what I love about you. You have this unique ability to take a screwed-up guy like me and turn him into something better. Half the things you've got me doing don't even make sense. I just turned down action and thriller roles to play the part of a single dad who falls in love with his son's teacher, because I like the heart and the message behind the movie. And next week, I'm meeting with a lawyer to discuss how I can start a charity to help kids caught in custody battles. I spent one hour after my lunch with Dallas yesterday, signing autographs and taking selfies with fans on the street. Like, what is even happening?

"I'm unrecognizable from the man I once was, which is great because I'm not even sure I liked that old version of myself. And I know the change is all because of you. Your goodness rubs off on people. You've made me a better man, given me hope for things that I've never dared hope about. And the best part is, you don't tell me to change in order to fit in with your life; you just accept me for who I am."

"I don't know if that's one hundred percent accurate. You were already a good man before you ever met me. You just never gave yourself any credit."

"It took being with you to see that I can be more. I can *want* more for myself."

"You can want more for yourself, and I want that for you, but it's hard for me to trust. What happens when you wake up two years from now and change your mind? When all the newness wears off, and you realize I'm nothing special, will you still feel the same? Will you still stay?"

"I won't change my mind."

"You don't know that."

"I know that I wouldn't promise you something right now if I weren't one hundred percent sure that I could follow through. I'm not saying it will be easy. But if I say I'm not going to get scared and leave you, then you can trust that."

"I've just had my heart broken so many times. I don't see how, in one week, out of the blue, you can go from not knowing what you want to wanting a long-term, committed relationship. It doesn't add up."

"Jenna, I'm trying here!" I groan. "I'm opening myself up in ways I never have before so I don't lose you. Stop getting in my way. Help me." I take another step forward, reaching for her hand. "Help me hold onto us. Because I can't do it alone. I need you to believe that I can do it."

Her eyes water over, but no actual tears drop. "I want to believe you."

"Then do." My hand caresses her cheek, brushing her hair back. "I care more about your happiness than anything else. And I'm not going to stop fighting for us, because I really do think we can make it. That's the craziest sentence I've said in my whole life. But I said it." I take her other hand in mine so we're holding both hands. "You want a man that loves you for you, someone that completely adores Jenna Lewis, not the girl they see in the magazines or the one they see on the TV screen. Well, that's me. I love the real Jenna Lewis. I don't care about any of the fake stuff. Being real with the real you is better than any fake scenario. And I know I said that I didn't want to spend my life with one person, but I think that's because I'd never found anyone who made the risky stuff seem worth it. But then I got to know you, and now I can actually picture a future together. I *want* a future together.

"I just want to deserve you, and I think I finally do, so don't ruin this because you're scared you can't trust me. I'm scared too, but I'm here. I'm ready to be the man you need, so let me take care of you. Let me show you what it's like to fully be loved, and you can show me what it's like to believe in something worth holding on to."

Her eyes drop, and she sucks in a deep breath before looking back at me. "I want the fantasy. Like, the whole thing —marriage, kids, happily ever after. It's too soon to know if that's right for us, but if we're going to try this relationship for real, you need to know that's the goal. It's all on the table."

"I know. Did you not just listen to my speech?"

"Yes, but I need to clarify so we're on the same page and there's no confusion."

"There's no confusion. I know what I'm getting myself into." I grimace. "That sounded bad. I just mean I understand your needs, and I want to meet them. Which reminds me…" I let go of her hands and reach into my back pocket. "I made you something." I hand her an envelope.

Her fingers slide over the paper, opening the flap. "What's this?"

"I'm auditioning for the part of the man in your life, and this is a list of my qualifications." I scratch the top of my head, suddenly feeling insecure about my idea. "I mean, a list of qualifications about myself would normally be stupid, but since we just finished filming *The Promised Prince,* and Trev wrote Renna a list, I thought I could do it too."

Her lips slowly grow into a smile. "You made me a list like Trev did for Renna?"

"Yes, but instead of being things that I wanted to talk to you about, it's qualifications of why I deserve to have the role as the man in your life."

"Okay." Jenna finally smiles big, something I've been dying to see this whole time. She spreads the paper apart, and my heart starts pounding as I watch her read my list.

JENNA

1. I'm pretty big and strong, so I can be your in-house security team all the time. Emphasis on *in-house* and *all the time*.

2. Everybody already thinks we're together, so it's easy to just keep going.

3. You've seen me at my worst and still seem to somewhat like me.

4. I promise to always be your biggest supporter and fan.

5. I know exactly how you like to be held.

6. Each time we play twenty questions, I keep getting better and better at answering questions. Plus, I won't tell anyone that you're the official spokesperson for the game. Your secret is safe with me.

7. I can't do math, which means you'll constantly get to show off how smart you are by doing math for me.

8. I think you're more beautiful than any woman I've ever seen. And it's not because you're a model or because you look exceptionally good with very little clothes on. I think you're beautiful because you hold so much goodness in your smile and the way you treat other people.

9. I can't say for certain, but I'm pretty confident you like the way I smell. I've caught you sniffing me about a hundred times while filming.

10. I've seen your most embarrassing moment, so if you stay with me, you won't have to relive it just to tell some other guy.

11. I love the way you greet people. Did you know you greet people differently than everyone else? Well, you do, and it's the cutest thing I've ever seen.

12. I'm in awe of your talent when it comes to film-making and think that you should try your hand at directing.

13. I have the most exquisite chest, arms, and six-pack you've ever seen. An arrogant, bad-boy persona that you find wildly attractive. And I'm a good kisser. I know we've been through all of this already, but since this is a list of my qualifications, I thought it was important to mention those things again.

14. I adore you. Like, *really* adore every little thing you do. Your smile, your laugh, the way you brush your hair back from your face…I adore it all and I promise to let everyone else know how I feel about you.

15. We were slow, but we found our chemistry. No, we found explosive chemistry, and I think that deserves a spot on this list. I dare you to find another man that you have more chemistry with than me. I mean, I'm not actually daring you. Really, I just want you to choose me.

16. Dave. I've never even met Dave, but the fact that I was enormously jealous of him and disappointed when I thought he was your boyfriend and not just some good guy who helps you do charity work tells me my heart one hundred percent belongs to you.

17. I don't recognize you when you wear big sunglasses, so I'll keep you humble, which maybe you need since everyone else seems to recognize you every-where we go.

18. I'll never take you for granted. I'll cherish you every day, walk in the shadows so you can shine, open your door for you, hold your hand, tell you every day how special you are, listen when you talk, and make you the center of my entire world.

19. I'll be the man that you've always hoped for and give you the happy ending you deserve.

20. But my best qualification: I love you. More than I love myself or anything else. You come first.

I SWIPE a tear off my cheek and look up at Cody, expecting to see anxiety over me reading his words, but instead, I see devotion and so much love behind his blue eyes.

"There are twenty qualifications," I say, holding up the paper.

"It's kind of an important number for us."

"This is a pretty convincing list of qualifications."

"I think so. Put it up against any other man, and I don't think he'd stand a chance."

"When it comes to you, Cody, *I* didn't stand a chance. My

heart was always going to be yours no matter how hard I fought it. But I don't want to fight it anymore. I want to believe that you can be everything you say, and I know you can, because you've shown me who you really are. You've shown me what it's like to be respected, and cherished, and wanted for more than just my body. I've never had that before, but I have it with you."

He leans forward, lowering his voice. "Just as a sidenote, I also really enjoy your body, but it's not the main thing. I like all the other stuff about you more. But I just wanted to be honest." He takes a step back, like he's giving me the space I need to finish my speech.

I laugh, rolling my eyes. "Relationships aren't just about the emotional connection. I also want you to want me physically."

"Trust me. There's no problem there. Not a single one. Add it to my list of qualifications."

"Okay, I will." I smile, loving the way his searing gaze makes me blush. "The truth is, I always hoped that we'd make it, that the fake relationship would turn into a real one."

"You did?"

"Against my better judgment, but yes, that's what I hoped. And now, here you are, offering me everything I ever wanted. And the best part is, I feel the same way. I love you too."

He smiles, pressing his hand against his heart—something I've seen him do many times. But tonight, in the glow of my front porch light, Cody Banner has never looked more handsome. "I don't think anyone has ever said that to me before and really meant it."

"I mean it." I wrap him in a hug. "Cody, I love you."

His nose buries into my neck as his hold around my body tightens. We stand there for a minute, wrapped in each other's arms, letting our broken hearts melt away into something more beautiful.

I pull back, gazing into his eyes. "You once told me that

everyone leaves you because you don't add value. That's wrong. You add value in the quiet way you support people and how you build others up. You've taken my broken heart and made me whole. You're invaluable to me." His eyes water over in the most tender way. "I won't leave you, or make you a pawn in a game, or anything like what your parents did. Together we'll fight to make this relationship last."

"I'm in if you're in," Cody says, but his words get lost as his lips press to mine.

His kiss is sweet, a tender seal on everything spoken. It's different than other kisses I've had in my life. It's gentle and sentimental, a physical declaration of all the things Cody promises and, in return, all the things I feel too. A kiss like this is more powerful than any other. It transcends our physical connection, bringing us emotionally closer together than anything else ever has.

Cody pulls back. "Just to clarify, I got the part as the man in your life, right?"

I laugh. "Yes, you got the part."

He slings his arm around my shoulder. "Good, because I wasn't going to leave here until you gave it to me. I'm clearly the best guy for the role."

"Clearly."

We start walking toward the house.

"You must be exhausted," Cody says, pulling my hip against his as we walk together. "Being the gentleman that I am, I'm going to take you straight to bed."

My head falls back with laughter. "Such a gentleman."

"Yep, I'm going to get you out of these clothes, put you in bed, *tuck* you in." His nose nuzzles into the side of my neck as we climb the front steps.

"What about you? You took a pretty hard fall off my gate. Maybe I should put you to bed, nurse your wounds."

He holds his side dramatically as I unlock the front door and twist the handle.

"You know, that does sound necessary. If you want to play the part of a nurse, I'm a willing participant in any plan you have."

I turn and face him, grabbing his hand as I walk backward inside my house. "Play the part of a nurse?"

"Role-playing seems to be a strength of ours."

"No more role-playing." I laugh, shaking my head. "I'm ready for everything to be real."

Cody pulls me in. "Then real is what you're going to get."

He kisses me again, kicking the front door shut with his foot.

EPILOGUE

FIVE YEARS LATER: HOLLYWOOD
WALK OF FAME

CODY

THE PHOTOGRAPHERS ARE AGGRESSIVE
TODAY.

"Jenna! On your left!"

"Jenna, pivot!"

"Jenna, touch the star!"

"Jenna! Straightforward."

"Ms. Lewis, over here!"

Everyone wants a piece of Jenna. Why wouldn't they? Being the fastest female actor to receive a star since her debut role is a pretty big deal.

Heck, I don't even have a Hollywood Star yet. Not that I'm complaining. I'm more than happy to be in the shadows as my beautiful wife kneels next to a star with her name engraved across it on the sidewalk of Hollywood Boulevard.

I'm proud of Jenna and all she's accomplished in her acting career after *The Promised Prince*.

Two tiny hands press against my beard, squishing my cheeks toward my mouth in the most unflattering way.

Maggie giggles. "Daddy, ugly."

Two-year-old honesty is brutal.

I scrunch my nose together, widen my eyes, and stick my tongue out, adding to the ugliness.

Maggie's head falls back with more bubbly giggles.

"Let's get some pictures of the whole family," one photographer shouts.

Jenna straightens from her spot by her star, looking over at me and Maggie.

I pull her little hands off my cheeks. "It's Maggie's turn for princess pictures."

She wiggles out of my lap and runs to Jenna, hopping and stomping on the star. The photographers love this, and a million more snaps and clicks go off.

I stand and turn to Trey, who's holding Dawson.

"Are you ready for this handoff?" Trey gently places the newborn into my arms, eliciting oohs and ahhs from the watching crowd.

I walk to Jenna, wondering if it would be inappropriate to hold my one-month-old baby in the air like Simba. As tempting as my own personal *Lion King* moment is, I opt for keeping the infant tucked in the crook of my arm.

"I feel like I'm leaking breast milk," she says into my ear when I sidle up next to her. "Will you check?"

My lips lift. "I would love to look at your chest. You don't have to ask me twice."

She nudges my side with a playful laugh.

"I'm kidding." I take a discreet look down, then flip my gaze back to her face with a subtle shake of my head.

"Oh, thank goodness. Can you imagine those pictures?" Jenna takes Dawson from my arms, positioning him forward for the cameras.

I guess I'm on Maggie duty.

I reach my hand out to the toddler as if that's going to be an effective strategy for reigning in the strong-willed child. "Come by Daddy."

The watching crowd laughs as she ignores my pleas,

starting up every parent's least favorite game: You can't catch me. I didn't even know this game existed, which is crazy since every child seems to be an expert at it.

"Maggie, sweetheart," Jenna tries. "Come smile at the cameras."

Maggie shakes her head, bouncing her blonde curls.

I dive forward, grabbing her arm. "Gotcha!" She laughs at first, and I feel like the best dad ever for getting her without a big scene. I hold her on my hip, pointing to the cameras.

"Kneel! Kneel!" the photographers shout.

Jenna and I obey, crouching down in front of the star.

"No!" Maggie whines and presses against my hold.

"Oh, no. She's not having it." Jenna laughs as cameras snap and capture the beginnings of my toddler's meltdown.

I don't know what to do. Do I make her stay for family pictures in front of the star at the risk of screaming and crying, or do I let her free? This is literally my worst nightmare.

"I'd like to trade," I say to Jenna as I wrestle Maggie. "How about I take the newborn that doesn't move?"

Jenna smiles back at me with an amused look. "You're doing great."

Doing great?

A two-year-old has somehow broken out of my stronghold and is slithering off my lap like a limp rag doll, and there's nothing I can do about it.

Maggie finishes her descent by steamrolling over the star, and before I can stop her, she's on her feet running away.

The lady from the Walk of Fame committee leans in. "Why don't we take some shots of Jenna with the Lewis family to give your daughter a break?"

With permission to be released, I go after Maggie, who is circling the makeshift red carpet stage as fast as her little legs will take her. I will not get myself in a run-down, going round and round with a two-year-old. I'd like to walk away from this event with some dignity.

Maggie makes it to the stage stairs. I immediately know what she's after. She reaches for the portable microphone on the lower shelf of the podium. Her slobbery mouth covers the top, and she yells into it. The crowd laughs, and I smile even though I'm dying inside.

"Maggie?" I keep my smile intact. "Can Daddy have the microphone?"

She runs to the other side of the stage, and my heart rate climbs with the fear that she's going to go off the side, falling to her three-foot death. But Jenna's there, catching her little body as she jumps off the edge into her mother's arms. They twirl, and suddenly, all of my anxiety washes away as I watch my better half in every way spin my daughter around.

I can't believe there was ever a time I didn't want *this*.

Was scared of *this*.

Creating and belonging to a family filled every hole and wound inside my heart. Five years ago, when I first started to fall in love with Jenna, I thought that I was a changed man. I thought that she had made me better. But each day, month, and year I spend next to her, I become a better version of myself. Jenna taught me how to trust in love and commitment. She's given me everything that makes me happy.

I walk over to my girls, noticing Jenna's mom behind them, holding Dawson.

I place a gentle kiss on Maggie's cheek. "You like making Daddy look silly, don't you?"

She nods her head up and down while banging her hand against the top of the microphone.

I tug Jenna into me for a side hug, wrapping my arm around her waist. Maggie's body smashes between us. "When you envisioned your five-year plan, did you see all of this? Me running around, chasing our kids while you get a Hollywood Star?"

Her head pulls back, and her green eyes glimmer. "No." She smiles. "This is way better than what I planned."

"Same." I kiss her lips, hearing the clicks of cameras.

Then, a microphone hits the top of my head.

THE END

I hope you enjoyed Cody and Jenna's story. I love hearing what readers liked most about my books, so don't forget to leave a review and tell me.

Join my newsletter at www.kortneykeisel.com for giveaways and to hear about my upcoming books. Stay connected with me on Instagram, Facebook, or Pinterest

Did you know that The Promised Prince, the series that Cody and Jenna star in, is one of my real books?
Read it on Amazon.

ALSO BY KORTNEY KEISEL

Famously In Love (Romantic Comedy)

Why Trey Let Me Get Away

How Jenna Became My Dilemma

The Sweet Rom "Com" Series

Commit

Compared

Complex

Complete

Christmas Books (Romantic Comedy)

Later On We'll Conspire

The Holiday Stand-In

The Desolation Series (Dystopian Royal Romance)

The Rejected King

The Promised Prince

The Stolen Princess

The Forgotten Queen

The Desolate World

ACKNOWLEDGMENTS

Each time I finish a book, I'm so thrilled, but things felt different when I finished How Jenna Became My Dilemma. I was thrilled, yes, but I was also relieved and amazed. I may have even shed a tear or two when I sent it off to my editor. The book took a lot out of me to write. I was slow and needed help figuring out where I wanted to take it. Many times I didn't think I would finish and debated canceling my pre-order even after I pushed the release date back.

Enter Madi.

She texted me out of the blue, asking how the story was going when I'd been praying for help with this book. She was literally an answer to my prayers. She read what I had and encouraged me to keep going. She also Marco Polo'd me back and forth brainstorming ideas. Her brilliant mind came up with the concept of using The Promised Prince as the series Jenna and Cody were working on. At first, I wasn't sure if I could pull that idea off, but after a few days of thinking about it, it was another answer to my prayers. In addition to being awesome about the book, Madi texted me randomly just to check in to see if I was hitting my word count goals. She also would do math in her head and tell me exactly how many words I needed to write per day in order to actually finish the book. She popped on the document and read chapters as I wrote them, and basically was a rock star. So Madi, I cannot thank you enough for everything you did for me. You are truly an amazing friend that I can count on. Thanks for always having my back. I love you!

A huge thanks goes out to my sister, Stacy. She's so busy and somehow found the time to beta read for me. Her opinions and influence are invaluable to me. She just gets plot and character motivation and confirms when things are stupid in the story in a way nobody else can. I completely trust her. Stacy, thanks again for being a part of another book with me. You're the best!

I want to thank my other beta readers: Meredith, Chelsea, and Meg. You guys were so awesome to get the book read in such a short amount of time, and your feedback was seriously crucial to making this book what it is. Thanks for being there for me and for your honesty. I really appreciate it.

Thank you to my critique group: Martha, Kasey, and Ashley. I'm sure you got tired of reading so many different versions of the same chapter, but you were such good sports about it. I love your feedback and sincerely appreciate your friendship even more.

Kylee, thanks for lending me your epic, embarrassing wrap pants story. I hope I did it justice. It's literally one of the funniest stories I've ever heard, and I am honored to have it in my book.

Jenn, you are the best editor ever. You're always willing to work around my crazy timeframe, changes, and missed deadlines. Thank you so much for all of the work you did on this book.

Melody, I absolutely love this cover design. You're the best to work with and have completely spoiled me with your talents.

To my readers--you are all the best. Thanks for your patience, especially when I pushed the release date back. I appreciate your excitement, reviews, word of mouth, shares, and all the ways you support me as a writer. It is humbling to have so many people who read my books and make it possible for me to keep doing this Thank you! Thank you!

My family was so supportive, especially during the last few weeks of trying to get this book done and to the editor. Thank you to Kurt for all the Crumbl cookies and for picking up the slack at home. Thank you to my kids for being patient and cheering me on. I love you all so much.

I know this book wouldn't have happened without the help of my Heavenly Father and Jesus Christ. I've never prayed so hard for help during a book than I did during this one. I was stuck and was blessed enormously to make it through, hit my word count, come up with ideas, and stay sane. I'm so grateful for all my blessings and to have another book done and out in the world.

ABOUT THE AUTHOR

Kortney loves all things romance. Her devotion to romance was first apparent at three years old when her family caught her kissing the walls (she attributes this embarrassing part of her life to her mother's affinity for watching soap operas like Days of Our Lives). Luckily, Kortney has outgrown that phase and now only kisses her husband. Most days, Kortney is your typical stay-at-home mom. She has five kids that keep her busy cleaning, carpooling, and cooking.

Writing books was never part of Kortney's plan. She graduated from the University of Utah with an English degree and spent a few years before motherhood teaching 7th and 8th graders how to write a book report, among other things. But after a reading slump, where no plots seemed to satisfy, Kortney pulled out her laptop and started writing the "perfect" love story...or at least she tried. Her debut novel, The Promised Prince, took four years to write, mostly because she never worked on it and didn't plan on doing anything with it.

Kortney loves warm chocolate chip cookies, clever song lyrics, the perfect romance movie, analyzing and talking about the perfect romance movie, playing card games, traveling with her family, and laughing with her husband.